GOD BE WITH US

GOD BE WITH US

A Daily Guide to Praying for Our Nation

QUIN SHERRER AND RUTHANNE GARLOCK

WARNER BOOKS

An AOL Time Warner Company

The authors are represented by Ann Spangler and Associates, 1420 Pontiac
Road, S.E., Grand Rapids, MI 49506.

For a prayer guide for praying for U.S. government officials, see the Web site
for Intercessors for America at *www.ifa-usapray.org* or write to Intercessors
for America, Box 447, Leesburg, VA 20177 or call 1-800-USA-PRAY.

Warner Books, Inc., 1271 Avenue of the Americas, New York, NY 10020
Visit our Web site at www.twbookmark.com.
For information on Time Warner Trade Publishing's online publishing
program, visit www.ipublish.com.

 An AOL Time Warner Company

Printed in the United States of America
First Warner Books printing: November 2001
10 9 8 7 6 5 4 3 2 1

ISBN: 0-446-53087-5
LCCN: 2001096614
Text design by Stanley S. Drate/Folio Graphics Co. Inc.

Dedicated to the memory of the thousands of Americans and those from other nations who perished in the terrorist attacks on our soil on September 11, 2001.

Even though I walk through the valley of the shadow of death,
I will fear no evil, for you are with me;
Your rod and your staff, they comfort me.

PSALM 23:4

Fifteen percent of the profits from this book will be donated to The September 11th Fund of The New York Community Trust and The United Way of New York City, c/o The New York Community Trust, 2 Park Avenue, New York, NY 10016. The purpose of the fund is to help address the immediate and longer-term needs of victims, their families, and communities affected by the events of September 11, 2001.

CONTENTS

1
GOD BE WITH US

2
SEEKING GOD'S FACE

3
PRAYING FOR OUR NATION AND ITS PEOPLE

4

PRAYING FOR OUR NATIONAL LEADERS

5

PRAYING FOR OUR FAMILIES

6

PRAYING FOR OUR STATE AND COMMUNITY LEADERS

7

PRAYING FOR OUR SPIRITUAL LEADERS AND CHURCHES

8

PRAYING FOR OUR FRIENDS, NEIGHBORS, AND COWORKERS

9

PRAYING FOR OUR ENEMIES

10

PRAYING FOR PERSONAL PEACE AND PROTECTION

11

HOW TO PRAY EFFECTIVELY

ACKNOWLEDGMENTS

We give grateful thanks to our husbands, LeRoy Sherrer and John Garlock.

Thanks also to Ann Spangler; Linda Peterson Kenney; Nancy Kennedy; Quinett Sherrer Simmons; Diane and Charles Gyurko; our editor, Leslie Peterson; Warner vice president Rolf Zettersten; and all our dedicated prayer partners.

It is only with the encouragement, prayers, and help of all these special friends that we were able to complete the project.

THE DAY THE WORLD
STOPPED TO PRAY

On September 11, 2001, when terrorist suicide pilots destroyed the New York World Trade Center and attacked the U.S. Pentagon, another "day of infamy" took its place in our nation's history. But although the horror of it left us numb with shock, people quickly began to respond. They volunteered to help in every conceivable way, even as the death toll rose and hope of finding more than a few survivors dwindled.

My son, Bradley, arrived back at his home in Manhattan in the wee hours of the morning on that unforgettable Tuesday. He was still asleep when the attack began about two miles south of his place in the Chelsea district. One of his apartment mates woke him with the news. The three young men who share the apartment scrambled to the roof of their building just in time to see the second tower implode upon itself. When my husband reached Bradley on his cell phone a few minutes later he was almost hysterical over what he'd just witnessed.

Over the next two days Bradley's emotions ran the gamut—disbelief, depression, anger, frustration, tears. On Thursday afternoon he called to say he and a friend planned to drive to Florida for a few days to get away from the whole scene, since all his work assignments had been cancelled. But late that evening the phone rang again.

It was Bradley on his cell phone, weeping almost uncontrollably. "Are you okay?" I said. No response. "Where are you?" I asked anxiously.

Finally, when he could speak, he said, "I'm at Ground Zero," meaning the twin towers rescue site. Then he told me he and four of his friends, after hours of watching the television coverage, had determined they would do something to help the rescue effort. They had decided to go down to the site and take food to the workers.

They packed up two small barbecue grills and whatever food they could find, then went out and bought more, including charcoal. Walking south, they stopped at restaurants and shops along the way, telling the managers where they were going and asking for food—and they got quite a bit. At Canal Street, where security was tight, one of them found a hole in a fence. They sneaked through one at a time and scattered, then reconnected through cell phone calls. They found a corner four blocks from the rescue site near a spot where workers went to detoxify their gear by hosing off the asbestos dust and ashes. It was the last street where the street lights were still working, and the closest they could get to where the twin towers had once stood.

Setting up the two grills on the curb, they started cooking and made an assembly line to put the burgers together. No one was around when they started, but word spread quickly among the workers that food was nearby. The "official" place for them to go for food was several blocks away. Bradley said the workers didn't want to go that far; they wanted to hurry and grab something to eat, then rush back. He was overwhelmed to see these men, already exhausted from hours of work, grab a burger and head back to the site.

"Mom, we made 150 hamburgers, and expected to be feeding people into the night," he said. "But all our food was gone in one hour!" Then he broke down and began sobbing. "There's no more food, and those people are hungry!"

By this time I was crying, too, and telling him how proud I was of him.

"But it's not enough!" he said, and began to weep again.

"Bradley, we can never do enough," I reminded him. "That's why we have to pray—but at least you did *something!*" Then I asked about his plans for going to Florida.

"I'm not going anywhere," he said. "No way am I leaving New York. I'm alive and walking around! These people need help, and I have to help them. You can't believe what it's like down here, Mom. It's a war zone."

My own family had suddenly become involved in this tragedy—it was no longer a distant news report. I assured Bradley of my love and prayers, and he quickly hung up to preserve his cell phone battery. I immediately began praying with renewed fervor for my son and his friends and for everyone involved in the rescue effort. I asked God to grant wisdom to our national leaders as they grappled with the tough decisions they would need to make because of the attack.

Probably most of us yearn to help in some tangible way under such circumstances; after Bradley's call I wrote a check to the Salvation Army. The next day Bradley couldn't get back to Ground Zero. So he gathered up writing tablets and file folders he had on hand and took them to the Armory in Manhattan to pass out to hundreds of people waiting in lines to register information about their missing loved ones.

The headline on my local newspaper today was "World Stops to Pray." Yesterday our president called us to prayer, and now even politically correct media spokesmen talk openly about prayer. We feel strongly that one of the greatest contributions we can make is to pray for our nation, its leaders, and its people. And not just during crisis, but on a regular basis. In this little book you will find prayers and devotionals to help guide you in praying for our nation, our leaders, and our families.

We urge you to join us as we pray, "God be with us."

RUTHANNE GARLOCK
September 15, 2001

1

GOD BE WITH US

The only thing we have to fear is fear itself . . . We face arduous days that lie before us in the warm courage of national unity; with the clear consciousness of seeking old and precious moral values . . . In this dedication of a nation we humbly ask the blessing of God. May He protect each and every one of us! May He guide me in the days to come.

FRANKLIN DELANO ROOSEVELT, IN HIS FIRST
INAUGURAL ADDRESS, JULY 2, 1932

Today, as American flags wave from our homes and office buildings almost seventy years after our nation faced the Great Depression, followed by World War II, we again face arduous days in the war against terrorism. We are a people trying to cope with loss, trying to live our lives more fully as we begin the process of grieving and healing. All across the country, church doors are open for people to come any time to pray. Herein lies the strength of our country. Herein lies our hope for tomorrow—calling on God for help. May he again be with us to guide us into the future.

We Need God's Comfort

My eyes fail, looking for your promise;
I say, "When will you comfort me?" . . .
I have suffered much;
Preserve my life, O Lord, according to your word.

PSALM 119:82, 107

When disasters such as the recent terrorist attacks strike our nation, a mysterious bonding seems to occur among those who experience the event. Our disagreements and differences suddenly aren't so important anymore. We stand on common ground.

"It is encouraging that faced with unspeakable grief the country has turned to the only one capable of getting us through this—God," stated an editorial in *The Lariat* at Baylor University in Waco, Texas. "What is also remarkable is that our differing faiths have not been a barrier to the country as it united to seek God."[1]

Over and over throughout our nation's history we've seen Americans come together like this—when war is declared against us . . . when a president is assassinated . . . when floods, earthquakes, hurricanes, or tornados occur . . . or when terrorists kill innocent citizens. Suddenly, in the face of such threats, once self-absorbed people begin reaching out to help one another. We are willing to make sacrifices and go beyond the call of duty. Yet we quickly realize we never can do enough. That's when we join our voices with loved ones and neighbors to cry out to God for help and comfort.

On September 11, in New York City and all across the land, churches opened for prayer and people gathered to find solace in one another. Students at Hope College in Holland, Michigan, gathered to sing hymns, and thousands of students at the University of Texas in Austin held a spontaneous campus candlelight vigil. A pastor in Houston said his first thought was to go somewhere and pray alone. Then he thought, "What about the others? And what better place to grieve than a church? There's nobody to turn to like God. So we called a prayer meeting."[2]

Ministers of a midtown Manhattan church stood on the sidewalk inviting passersby to stop and pray; some three hundred people gathered at one point.

"The cynics aren't stopping, but lots of people are," said Dr. William Shillady of New York. "Right now, nobody's being negative about the church . . . people are experiencing us in a unique way. I do hope that somehow, some good will come out of this, that somehow, people's lives may change."[3]

Clearly the life of every American changed on September 11. The sad fact is too often we don't experience such a level of bonding with others until tragedy strikes. Now we must choose to be sensitive to the needs around us rather than insulating ourselves against them. One rabbi urged his people to "find the strength to rise and walk on."[4] God promises to give us his strength, and as we receive it from him we can use it to comfort others.

PRAYER

Lord, I am grieved by what has happened to our nation. I will never forget the images of violence I have seen. They are so vivid, replayed over and over on television. I can't stop thinking about those who died and those who survived—please comfort them and their families. And Lord, please lift this heaviness from me. Help me to see that above the rubble stands the Rock—the only One who is forever. Hold my hand as I reach out to comfort those who are grieving over this tragedy. Help my life to count—I want to be a light on the path of darkness. Amen.

God Has Blessed Us

The people who know their God will firmly resist.

DANIEL 11:32

School children sing it, as do sports spectators, executives, school teachers, policemen, and citizens from every walk of life. It is the one song that unites people throughout the land and stirs their hearts like no other. That song is our national anthem and it has a story that is as patriotic as the stars and stripes themselves.

The War of 1812 pitted the United States and its volunteer forces against Great Britain's well-trained soldiers and the most powerful navy in the world. The British attacked and captured Washington, D.C., burning the Capitol building, the White House, and other government buildings. Next, they sought to capture Baltimore, an important port and America's third largest city at the time.

By the time the British reached Baltimore, Americans had strengthened their defenses around Fort McHenry. Old ships waited in the shallow water around the fort to be sunk in an effort to prevent the British fleet's entry into the port.

Francis Scott Key, a thirty-five-year-old American lawyer, had come from Washington, D.C., to Baltimore with a letter from President James Madison appealing to the British admiral of the attacking fleet to release an American he was holding, Dr. William Beanes. The admiral finally agreed to free the doctor, but only after the battle was over. So from its position in Chesapeake Bay, the admiral's British warship, with Key and Dr. Beanes aboard, bombarded the American Fort McHenry that memorable night of September 14, 1814. Throughout the night, as rockets glared and bombs burst, Mr. Key wondered who was winning the battle. Clouds of smoke hung over the battered fort and he strained to see through the haze. Was the flag that flew over the fort the Union Jack or the banner with fifteen stars and fifteen stripes—America's symbol?

When the smoke of battle finally lifted and morning dawned, young Francis spotted "Old Glory" still waving over the fort. On the back of an envelope he wrote a few lines of poetry describing the scene. Later that night, in his hotel room in Baltimore, he finished the poem. The words were joined with the tune of a traditional English hymn, and within weeks it was being sung across the country. On March 3, 1931, Congress officially declared it the national anthem of the United States.[5]

The fourth verse says:

O! thus be it ever when free men shall stand
Between their loved home and the war's desolation;
Blest with vict'ry and peace, may the Heav'n rescued land
Praise the Pow'r that hath made and preserved us a nation!
Then conquer we must, when our cause it is just;
And this be our motto, "In God is our trust."
And the star spangled banner in triumph shall wave
O'er the land of the free and the home of the brave![6]

What a message this song has for all Americans as our country is threatened once again, but by a different enemy.

PRAYER

Lord, thank you for brave men and women who have been pioneers for freedom. They have set us examples of true patriotism. May your hand continue to guide us and help us remain faithful to the purpose you have for our nation. Amen.

God Owns It All

Yours, O LORD, is the greatness and the power
And the glory and the majesty and the splendor,
For everything in heaven and earth is yours.
Yours, O LORD, is the kingdom;
You are exalted as head over all.
Wealth and honor come from you;
you are the ruler of all things.

1 CHRONICLES 29:11–12

How easily we forget that the possessions and treasures we have in this life are not truly ours—they belong to God. Yes, we work hard to provide shelter and sustenance for our children or others in our care. And we try as best we can to prepare for our own future security. But when setbacks and losses come, we sometimes feel it is God who has taken security from us.

Deprived or dispossessed? Not possible. Not if what we seem to lose is not really ours in the first place. Great minds have often described human possessions as "on loan" from God or "borrowed" by us. The same with our talents and abilities. And if we believe in eternal life, our time to use these physical endowments is comparatively very short indeed.

Materialism then is a distortion—an undue emphasis upon what in the long run has little significance. Author Philip Yancey called it "a belief that human life consists mainly (or solely) in what takes place here and now, in the world of matter."[7] Many feel that this emphasis on materialism is the main force driving our headlong pursuit of technology, conveniences, and commerce—and the impetus behind those that hate our nation and what it stands for. Suicide bombers struck the World Trade Center because to them it symbolized our nation's wealth. But instead of emphasizing materialism, this tragedy instead reminded us that our country's greatest asset does not reside on Wall Street but in the morality and courage of its citizens.

To always have God in proper perspective will protect us from the over-the-top materialism that threatens us. We know the pleasures and possessions of this world are nothing compared to gifts of family, friends, and faith. If we seek a relationship with God and rely on his provision, then we will have true confidence and security. As the gospel folk song says, "He's got the whole world in His hands."

✍

PRAYER

Lord, forgive us for embracing a materialistic way of life that leaves little room for anything else. We acknowledge that indeed you own it all, and we thank you for the blessings you give us. Help us to see that our time of physical life on earth is just the anteroom of eternity. Guide us in making decisions that perceive not just the now of our daily lives, but the forever of our future. May we live with this understanding always in mind. Amen.

Mysteries Remain

———— ⤳ ————

"For My thoughts are not your thoughts,
Nor are your ways my ways," says the LORD.
"For as the heavens are higher than the earth,
So are My ways higher than your ways,
And my thoughts than your thoughts."

ISAIAH 55:8–9

Have you ever felt so overwhelmed by difficulties and loss that you found yourself crying out, "God, I don't understand!"? We ask over and over, "Why does God allow this evil?" Despite stretching our human reasoning as far as it can go, we still cannot comprehend the ways of God. Perhaps we're even tempted to blame him for the problems besetting us. In such times we need to be reminded of God's words to Isaiah: "My ways are higher."

One of the greatest mysteries about God is that he created us with the power to choose. From the beginning he has given us free will. Adam and Eve made the wrong choice in the Garden, and the human race has contended with evil ever since. Yet God, who is full of mercy, has always provided salvation for all of us. When we confess and repent of our sins we receive his forgiveness.

Many of course choose to pursue their own evil ways and to not accept his free gift. Sometimes such people inflict immeasurable suffering and death upon others. History is strewn with tyrants like Nero, Genghis Khan, Pol Pot, Adolf

Hitler, Idi Amin, and Osama bin Laden. The actions of such evil men make us cry, "Why?"

Here is the awesome mystery, though: each of us is free to choose, and though we may choose the horrible rather than the honorable, God can yet lead us through it all to a final good result. Isn't Calvary itself the ultimate example? A heinous crime against the innocent becomes a vehicle of grace and blessing to the world. What a breathtaking mystery!

It was this enigma that inspired the eighteenth-century hymnwriter Charles Wesley to write:

He left His Father's throne above,
So free, so infinite His grace!
Emptied Himself of all but love,
And bled for Adam's helpless race.[8]

PRAYER

O God, we acknowledge the sins of our nation and confess that we have allowed the moral fiber of our society to become weak. But Lord, we ask you to forgive us and help us make choices according to your standards. Help us to love the things you love and hate the things you hate. Amen.

There Are Always Tragedies and Natural Disasters

———— ✄ ————

For he does not willingly bring affliction or grief to the children of men.

LAMENTATIONS 3:33

W hy do horrible things happen—especially to those who seem to deserve it the least? During his message at the memorial service for victims of the terrorist attacks, the Reverend Billy Graham expressed the same question. "I have been asked hundreds of times in my life why God allows tragedy and suffering. I have to confess that I really do not know the answer totally, even to my own satisfaction. I have to accept, by faith, that God is sovereign."

Indeed there are no satisfactory explanations, but author Elisabeth Elliot, whose husband, Jim, was murdered while serving in the mission field, says it's not necessarily wrong to ask the question, "Why?" She writes:

> There are those who insist that it is a very bad thing to question God. To them "why?" is a rude question. That depends, I believe, on whether it is an honest search, in faith, for his meaning, or whether it is a challenge of unbelief and rebellion. The psalmist often questioned God and so did Job. God did not answer the questions, but he answered the man—with the mystery of himself.[9]

What about natural disasters: hurricanes, earthquakes, tornadoes, floods, volcanic eruptions, drought? These are the things that are often referred to as "acts of God"—especially in insurance disclaimers. Since God is the Creator of the earth, the natural elements are under his control. But we don't believe he purposely sends disasters to afflict or bring grief to humans. Jesus declared that "He [God] causes his sun to rise on the evil and the good, and sends rain on the righteous and the unrighteous" (Matt. 5:45).

One recent spring, North Dakota was hit by a severe surprise blizzard. The snow storm devastated the region and even froze livestock to death. When the ice melted, the destruction became even more evident. A friend from Fargo wrote:

> Huge electric poles were snapped like toothpicks. All you could see for miles was water. We spent four days sandbagging our construction job sites and helping neighbors, only to return home late each evening to see television news reports of total destruction and even fires in parts of Grand Forks, farther north. Some said it was like being in a war zone, but we knew God was in control.
>
> Through it all, God was very close. I sometimes felt overwhelmed by the chaos of destruction, but never to the point of abandonment or despair. God's peace prevailed in the midst of the turmoil. The answers I prayed for didn't always come, but I learned in a deeper way the sovereignty of God. For a month our local radio station ran one minute messages by local pastors. Many hearts were open to God's help, and in God's mercy, Fargo and Grand Forks never lost one life.[10]

It is hard for us to comprehend these disasters—natural or personal—but we place our hope in God, in his sovereign grace. As Elisabeth Elliot affirms, he answers us "with the mystery of himself."

PRAYER

Lord, I know none of us can escape difficulties altogether. But with your help I want my attitude to be touched by your love and grace. Should a natural disaster come to my area, keep me from bitterness and show me how to reach out to help others in their distress.

2

SEEKING GOD'S FACE

Whereas it is the duty of all nations to acknowledge the providence of Almighty God, to obey His will, to be grateful for his benefits, and humbly to implore His protection and favor . . . Now, therefore, I do recommend and assign Thursday, the twenty-sixth day of November next, to be devoted by the people of these United States . . . That we then may all unite unto him our sincere and humble thanks for His kind care and protection of the people of this country . . . for the great degree of tranquility, union and plenty which we have enjoyed; for the peaceable and rational manner in which we have been enabled to establish constitutions of government for our safety and happiness . . . for the civil and religious liberty with which we are blessed . . . That we may then unite in most humbly offering our prayers and supplications to the great Lord and Ruler of Nations, and beseech Him to pardon our nation and other transgressions . . . to promote the knowledge and practice of the true religion and virtue.

GEORGE WASHINGTON, IN HIS PROCLAMATION FOR
A DAY OF PUBLIC THANKSGIVING AND PRAYER,
OCTOBER 3, 1789, FROM THE CITY OF NEW YORK

On reading the speeches and documents of America's founding fathers, it is clear that their worldview was rooted in an awareness of the need for dependence upon God. The proclamation of a National Day of Thanksgiving and George Washington's call for united prayer reminds us that at this critical time in our nation's history we again need to seek God.

The Problem of Greed

———— 〜 ————

One man gives freely, yet gains even more;
Another withholds unduly, but comes to poverty.
A generous man will prosper;
He who refreshes others will himself be refreshed.

PROVERBS 11:24–25

To be greedy means to gorge oneself with food even after hunger has been abated. Or to indulge oneself with far more possessions than truly necessary. To most people in the world, America is synonymous with wealth and indulgence.

I (Ruthanne) remember traveling with my husband in central Europe several years before the Iron Curtain fell. We arrived in Munich without our luggage because it had missed a connecting flight. We couldn't wait for our bags to catch up with us, though. After buying a few essentials in Vienna, we continued our journey with only our carry-on baggage. We drove across Austria, through Czechoslovakia, and on to Poland for a pastors' conference.

Our hosts in Poland received us warmly, but as I looked around their cramped, one-bedroom apartment, I wondered where we were going to eat or sleep. I soon discovered that the living room served several functions. A meal for seven people was served on the coffee table sitting in front of the sofa. When bedtime came, the woman of the house converted the sofa into a bed for us, explaining in her limited English that normally she and her husband slept here, but they would share their children's bedroom. Suddenly I was very glad we didn't have our big suitcases.

Though our host family seemed poor by American standards, their situation was typical of most people throughout the Soviet bloc nations at that time. Food was rather scarce, yet they seemed delighted to share with us the best they could afford. With great pride, our hostess served a dessert topped with fresh strawberries. I could only imagine the price she must have paid for them, both by putting a dent in her family's food budget and by standing in a long queue to buy them.

I returned from that trip—after our bags caught up with us near Hamburg—with a new appreciation for the blessings we enjoy in our nation. And a desire to find ways to reach out to those whose possessions are few, but who still exhibit a generous spirit. Despite the culture and language barriers, we felt at one with these Polish friends because of our common faith.

PRAYER

Lord, we are so easily overcome by greed and materialism, and we take for granted the many blessings you have bestowed on us. Please forgive us as a nation, Lord, and also forgive me personally. Help us to curb our selfishness and share more generously the blessings you have given us. Amen.

The Problem of Ease

The seed [the word of God] that fell among thorns stands for those who hear, but as they go on their way they are choked by life's worries, riches and pleasures, and they do not mature.

LUKE 8:14

Pleasure is a good thing—a gift from God. But like anything else, it can become an idol if we make it our primary goal. Giving pleasure first place in our hearts weakens our resolve to live for God. We become selfish and soft and uninterested in the things that are important to him. We use people and things, waste time and money, and fall prey to immorality, unbridled spending, gambling—even though they lead us perilously far from God.

I (Quin) have a friend who almost drowned while white-water rafting. Now, nothing is wrong with the exhilaration one gets from riding down the rapids. Except that day it was wrong for my friend. Several people had drowned that summer in those waters. Three strangers had tried to warn her that day—a nurse, a waitress, and a man who walked over to her car in the parking lot before she got in her raft. "Don't go," each one had pleaded. But she had persisted.

Within minutes of taking to the water, my friend's raft overturned, sucking her under water. Her leg became stuck in some tree roots, immobilizing her. She believed she was drowning. Then this Bible verse popped into her head: "And everyone who calls on the name of the Lord will be saved"

(Acts 2:21). She couldn't speak, but in her mind she repeated the name of God over and over. As she did, miraculously, her leg came free and she shot to the surface.

"Once I make a decision I want to follow through with it," my friend said later. "But I learned much through my near brush with death in turbulent waters. After I ignored cautions from three people, I realized I needed to listen more. Now I pray and check in with God about everything I do, even fun times."[1]

Worldly pleasures can be like those raging waters. Before we stick a toe in, they seem so alluring. But then they drag us down.

If you see yourself caught in the net of pleasure-seeking, it's not too late to cry out for help. Call on the Lord and he will certainly save you and restore your sense of value as to what is truly important in life.

≋

PRAYER

Lord, forgive us for allowing pleasure to take precedence over you and your plans for us. Give us wisdom to make wise choices in all areas of life. Amen.

The Problem of Disregard for Life

———— ⫸ ————

For you created my inmost being;
You knit me together in my mother's womb.
I praise you because I am fearfully and wonderfully made;
Your works are wonderful, I know that full well . . .
All the days ordained for me were written in your book
before one of them came to be.

PSALM 139:14, 16

When hundreds of airline passengers are murdered by suicidal hijackers—what a senseless disregard for life. When more than seven hundred people who worked for the same company lose their lives in one fell swoop—what a tragic waste of life. When one little village on Long Island loses twenty of its citizens—what a sad disrespect for life.

We look at the smoking jumble of blackened metal and concrete that used to be the World Trade Center and mourn all the precious people who perished. Sanctity of life. People created in the image of God swept away by madmen who care not for the sanctity of life.

Thomas Jefferson penned in our Declaration of Independence:

We hold these truths to be self-evident, that all men are created equal, that they are endowed by their Creator with certain unalienable rights; that among these are life, liberty and the pursuit of happiness.

What did those terrorists know of this? Nothing.

America is still grief stricken—and will be for some time. We all deplore these dastardly acts. But have we considered the ways our own culture disregards life? Gang-related killings . . . Drive-by shootings . . . Neglect of the elderly . . . Racial prejudice leading to the death of a man dragged behind a truck . . . The killing of illegal immigrants . . . A military officer murdered by a young man who just had to have his sports car. There are also those who are genuinely concerned about the casual approach we have toward abortion and even euthanasia.

What a senseless disregard for life. It does give us cause to examine our own hearts. To search our innermost emotions and beliefs. And to review the moral, ethical, and civil foundations of our nation.

✍

PRAYER

Lord, forgive me for the attitudes I have harbored that are less than godly. I have looked the other way at crimes that did not involve me personally, and I judged those committing them. I admit that I too have hateful and prejudicial ideas. Please forgive me for ways in which I have shown disregard for life. Amen.

The Problem of Prejudice

Peter began to speak: "I now realize how true it is that God does not show favoritism but accepts men from every nation who fear him and do what is right. You know the message God sent to the people of Israel, telling the good news of peace through Jesus Christ."

ACTS 10:34–36

Terrorist attacks on America, perpetrated by radical fringe Muslims, have spawned hundreds of cases of harassment and hate crimes against innocent Muslims living here—some by people claiming to be godly, upstanding citizens.

Sue, who lives across the street from a Muslim family, seldom crossed paths with the husband, the imam of the local mosque, or his wife, who was usually at work. But she often heard the loud cars, music, and voices of their teenagers and their friends. She would wave and say hello when she had occasion.

But after September 11 Sue noticed the house was mostly dark and things were very quiet.

Do they feel threatened because of his position at the mosque? she wondered.

The following Saturday Sue heard a poem on the car radio about being a single point of light for someone else. She felt God calling her to be that for her neighbors—to show them love. She said:

One of my errands took me to a greenhouse, where I selected a beautiful mum, and my husband and I took it across the street as soon as I returned. Our neighbor, who had just come out to mow the lawn, was gracious when we gave him the plant. We briefly explained that although there were tensions in the world, we were glad he and his family were our neighbors. He visibly brightened, vigorously shook our hands, and told us how much he appreciated us as neighbors.

After we left he planted the mum in his front yard. I've not yet spoken to the wife—I just don't see her that often. Yet I can see that beautiful purple plant in her yard, and I'm trusting God to use it to offer hope and love.[2]

In biblical times Jews and gentiles had almost no association with one another. But when Jesus came proclaiming a message of peace and salvation for everyone, he commissioned his followers to do the same. When Cornelius, a Roman military officer, asked the apostle Peter to come to his house to explain the gospel message, Peter had to overcome his prejudice toward gentiles—especially Romans. But he obeyed, and Cornelius and his household responded positively.

We often still struggle to overcome prejudice toward those of a different race, religion, or social status. We must work hard to instead show kindness to others—to everyone—without bigotry or discrimination.

PRAYER

Grant, O God, that your holy and life-giving Spirit may so move every human heart (and especially the hearts of the people of this land), that barriers which divide us may crumble, suspicions disappear, and hatreds cease; that our divisions be healed, we may live in justice and peace; through Jesus Christ our Lord.[3]

We Need God's Heart

Call to Me, and I will answer you, and show you great and unsearchable things, which you do not know.

JEREMIAH 33:3

"You don't realize how precious life is until it's measured in minutes," one survivor was overheard to say about the terrorist attack on the New York World Trade Center.

"We need to realize that each day could be our last," declared an editorial in a university student newspaper. "Not so we can live in fear and be paranoid of every dark shadow or plane flying overhead, but to do the opposite—fear nothing. Live each day to have no regrets."[4]

In the wake of the most damaging act of war ever carried out on U.S. soil, Americans became suddenly and painfully aware of how fragile life actually is. As a nation we had to realign our sense of values as we cried out to God for comfort and help.

Certain historic events in our nation are burned into our collective memory—freeze-framed in images that remain even when we close our eyes to escape the horror. On the morning of September 11, 2001, many of us recorded a gallery of such images in our minds that we'll never forget.

But layered over the mental images of destruction are pictures of people showing God's love to those in need. People waiting for hours to donate blood. Children raising money to buy insulated gloves for the workers clearing rubble. Chefs preparing food for the rescue workers. Airline employees giving shelter to travelers stranded in a shut-down airport.

One way we can show God's heart to others is by practicing the reciprocal commands in the Bible. We need to minister to one another. There are more than fifty "one anothers" in the New Testament. Here are a few. We should:

- pray for one another (James 5:16)
- love one another (John 13:34–35, Rom. 13:8, 1 John 3:23)
- accept one another (Rom. 15:7)
- be hospitable to one another (1 Peter 4:9)
- be kind to one another (1 Thess. 5:15)
- serve one another in love (Gal. 5:13)
- carry one another's burdens (Gal. 6:2)
- forgive one another (Eph. 4:32, Col. 3:13)
- stop passing judgment on one another (Rom. 14:3)
- have concern for one another (1 Cor. 12:25)
- honor one another (Rom. 12:10)
- encourage one another (1 Thess. 5:11, Heb. 10:25)

When interviewed on national television, Anne Graham Lotz, daughter of evangelist Billy Graham, made this statement:

> Our nation has been hit and devastated by this day of terror, and now I believe it is our choice as to whether we're going to implode and just disintegrate emotionally and spiritually, or whether we'll make the choice to be stronger. I think right now we have the opportunity to come through this spiritually stronger than we've been in the past because we turn to God.[5]

It is difficult for a sick person to evaluate accurately the progress of his own recovery. By the same token, it may not be easy for us as a nation to gauge our own spiritual temperature. But in the weeks following the attack we've seen an increase in people helping one another, churches working together, and more people praying and speaking openly of our need to call upon the Lord. Let us pray that our increased desire to seek him will not wane.

PRAYER

Father God, help us to seek your face and hear your heartbeat during these difficult days. We are so very blessed to be able to reach out to others who need to sense your love and care for them right now. Help us to be your hands extended to them. Amen.

3

PRAYING FOR OUR NATION AND ITS PEOPLE

But all of us—at home, at war, wherever we may be—are within the reach of God's love and power. We all can pray. We all should pray. We should ask the fulfillment of God's will. We should ask for courage, wisdom, for the quietness of soul which comes alone to them who place their lives in His hands.

HARRY S. TRUMAN, 1950

When terrorists attacked our nation on September 11, their obvious intent was to strike terror into the hearts of the American people. Instead, their infamous acts have had a unifying effect on our nation. We've come to appreciate more fully our military personnel, our firefighters and law enforcement officers—even public officials who didn't get our vote at the ballot box. As we try to recover we reach for hope, strengthen our resolve to reach out to others, and pray for our country as never before.

Comfort Those Who Grieve

———— ✀ ————

Comfort, comfort, my people, says your God.

ISAIAH 40:1

Our nation has undergone a period of mind-numbing loss and deep grieving. We are mourning lost loved ones, lost dreams, and a lost sense of security. But through our collective experience, we have also found a community of support.

To comfort means to console, to extend compassion, to sigh with one who mourns. Not just offering casual sympathy, but rather deep empathy. We are weeping with those who weep—listening to those who long to share their memories. Not one tear is wasted. Not one prayer goes unheard.

A national tragedy has a way of breaking down barriers that once divided us. Patriotism becomes a strong bond, drawing us together. Following the recent catastrophes that affected our citizens, people stopped others on the streets to talk and ask questions and sometimes to offer condolences. The same questions were asked over the phone: "Does anyone in your family live in New York or Washington, D.C.?" "Did you know anybody who is missing or dead?" Almost every one of us was touched in some way by this disaster. If we didn't personally know someone involved, then we heard about a friend who lost a friend.

So begins the process of comforting.

America moved on after Pearl Harbor. We moved on after

both world wars. We moved past our grief of losing President John F. Kennedy to an assassin's bullet on that never-to-be-forgotten November day. Somehow, some way, our nation will move on after the these horrific disasters we've experienced more recently. But we'll do it as we comfort and encourage one another. And yes, as we pray for our nation and for one another.

When a restaurant owner in California heard news of the attack on the New York World Trade Center, he ran out to where his customers were eating and said, "Let's pray for our nation." A pastor led them as they fell on their knees.

A beauty technician in Colorado brought out a picture of a mother hen shielding two baby chicks under her wings and told her clients, "This is how we need the Lord to shelter and comfort us."

A woman waiting for her car to be serviced in Washington, D.C., suddenly found herself holding hands in a circle of about twenty customers and workers as they prayed for America.

Those who have been through tragedies often have a special empathy for comforting victims who feel overwhelmed by grief. But all of us, whether we feel adequate for the task or not, can reach out to others around us. Often, the greatest gift we can give is our willingness to simply be there for them.

PRAYER

As Paul said in 2 Corinthians 1:3–4, "Praise be to the God and Father of our Lord Jesus Christ, the Father of compassion and the God of all comfort, who comforts us in all our troubles, so that we can comfort those in any trouble with the comfort we ourselves have received from God." Amen.

Unite Us

———— ✧ ————

How good and pleasant it is
When brothers live together in unity! . . .
For there the Lord bestows his blessing,
Even life forevermore.

PSALM 133:1, 3b

Back in 1893 a Massachusetts teacher, Katharine Lee Bates, visited Colorado Springs, Colorado. While taking in the glorious view from atop Pike's Peak she wrote a poem describing the majesty and vastness of our land. Some time later a music composition by Samuel A. Ward was joined to Miss Bates' poem and the song as we know it today was born. Here are some of the words:

O beautiful for spacious skies,
For amber waves of grain,
For purple mountain majesties
Above the fruited plain!
America! America!
God shed His grace on thee,
And crown thy good with brotherhood
From sea to shining sea.[1]

One biographer says that Miss Bates often remarked, "Unless we crown our good with brotherhood, of what lasting value are our spacious skies, our amber waves of grain, our mountain majesties or our fruited plains?" Then she would add, "We must match the greatness of our country with the goodness of personal godly living."[2]

Brotherhood (or sisterhood) is that sense of unity that bonds us Americans together despite our differences. We declare in our pledge of allegiance that we are "one nation under God, indivisible, with liberty and justice for all." As Americans we enjoy tremendous personal freedoms, but preserving those freedoms requires unity in the face of adversity.

"With a great price our ancestors obtained this freedom," wrote Elmer Davis, who served as head of the Office of War Information during World War II. "But that freedom can be retained only by the eternal vigilance which has always been its price."

Our founding fathers were keenly aware of the cost of freedom. And every time war is waged on a broad scale—anywhere in the world—we're again reminded of it. During the difficult days of World War I, "America the Beautiful" became immensely popular, encouraging pride and loyalty among Americans. Today, we still gather to wave flags and sing this song—as I (Quin) witnessed recently in my city on a busy street corner right under the shadow of Pike's Peak.

The important thing, as we express our patriotic feelings, is to remain on the alert. Our government and military leaders must be ever vigilant in protecting this nation, and we must be attentive in prayer as we do our part to unite America.

PRAYER

Lord, thank you for our freedom, and for the blessings you have heaped upon us. Help us to fulfill the responsibilities that come with these blessings. Unite us in heart and in purpose under your will. God, please shed your grace on us—from sea to shining sea.

Strengthen Our
Judicial System

For the LORD is righteous,
He loves justice;
Upright men will see his face.

PSALM 11:7

One of the roles attributed to God is that of Judge. He loves justice and always judges fairly. As the prophet Micah tells us, he requires us to act justly and to love mercy (Micah 6:8). But we are fallible and sinful and we don't always act justly. In spite of that, God has appointed human beings as earthly judges to administer justice.

The book of 1 Kings tells us that when Solomon was king of Israel, he showed his love for the Lord by walking according to the statutes of his father, David. As a result, the Lord appeared to Solomon in a dream and told him to ask for anything.

He answered, "Your servant is here among the people you have chosen, a great people, too numerous to count or number. So give your servant a discerning heart to govern your people and to distinguish between right and wrong. For who is able to govern this great people of yours?" (1 Kings 3:8).

Because Solomon's desire for discernment in administering justice pleased the Lord, he granted the king his request. He also gave him riches and honor, which he hadn't asked for. Years earlier, Solomon's father, King David, wrote several psalms extolling God's love of justice. Perhaps that's where Solomon learned of it.

In contrast is the parable Jesus told of a judge who neither feared God nor cared about people such as the woman who continually came to him, pleading for justice against her adversary. He finally gave her justice only to keep her from bothering him (Luke 18:1-5).

This story shows the difference between the justness of God as judge who brings about "justice for his chosen ones who cry out to him day and night" (Luke 18:7), and the unjust judge who had no regard for true justice.

As is evident in that parable, not everyone who is elected or appointed within a nation's judicial system performs his or her duties with godly integrity. Even so, all are put in position by God's design. As you focus your prayers on our nation's vast justice system, learn the names of each of the nine Supreme Court justices as well as your local judges, and pray for each by name. Pray for the attorney general and the thousands of federal agents who serve under him.

Pray that justice will not be perverted (Deut. 16:19), withheld (Deut. 27:19), mocked (Prov. 19:28), or denied (Ex. 23:6). Pray that justice will be followed (Deut. 16:20), maintained (Ps. 106:3), understood (Prov. 28:5), and sought after (Isa. 1:17).

Pray that each member of our nation's judicial system will not simply administer justice, but will love justice as God does.

PRAYER

Lord, we ask that you strengthen our judicial system and strengthen our justices. Give them a desire to act justly, to love mercy and to walk humbly with you, our God (Micah 6:8). Amen.

Strengthen Our Military

---- 〰 ----

Do not hide your face from your servant;
Answer me quickly, for I am in trouble.
Come near and rescue me;
Redeem me because of my foes.

PSALM 69:17–18

This psalm was uttered as a plea for God to have mercy and to save a nation's leader from a host of enemies. It appears that leader was under a vicious attack by a widespread conspiracy. Does the situation sound familiar? Even contemporary?

It's been more than a decade since the young men and women of America have been so focused on the military. Thoughts of the draft and Selective Service are on everyone's mind. Even though the draft for military service is currently inactive, young men have for years been required to register with the Selective Service within thirty days of their eighteenth birthday. Should the draft be activated, a lottery based on birthdays would determine the order in which registered men would be called up for active duty.

According to one Selective Service official, more than six thousand men registered via the internet on the day of the terrorist attack.[3]

"A lot of young kids come and join the Army because they are patriotic," said one recruiter. "Americans have a very deep and loyal streak. It doesn't necessarily come out, but when the chips are down, they do show it."[4]

Whether or not we have a family member who serves in the military, we have an obligation—no, a deep desire—to pray for those who do. We can pray for their protection and well-being, for them to be alert to danger, wise in their decisions, and most of all that they will establish a personal relationship with the Lord and learn how to hear his voice.

Both the Bible and inspired hymns give us ways to pray for our armed forces. One of the most popular hymns among the military, "Eternal Father, Strong to Save"—sometimes called The Navy Hymn—was played by Navy and Marine bands at the funeral for President John F. Kennedy. Written in 1860 by William Whiting, it includes a prayer for God's protection. Some of the words are:

> *O Trinity of love and pow'r*
> *Our brethren shield in danger's hour;*
> *From rock and tempest, fire and foe,*
> *Protect them wheresoe'er they go:*
> *Thus evermore shall rise to Thee*
> *Glad praise from air and land and sea.*[5]

Every time we see a newscast reporting military actions by our U.S. forces, it can serve as a reminder to pray for those who willingly put themselves in harm's way to serve our country. The least we can do is to serve them by upholding them in prayer.

PRAYER

Lord, we pray that you will place your hand of protection over those serving our country in the military. Be their strength, their hope, their defense. Give them a sense of destiny, a realization of their purpose in their individual roles. Lord, we ask you to bring them home safely to their families. Wrap them in your love.

Help Us Appreciate Our Heroes

―――― ✵ ――――

God is not unjust; he will not forget your work and the love you
have shown him as you have helped his people and continue to
help them.

HEBREWS 6:10

Heartache at its worst, but America at her best," a radio
commentator said in describing the days following
September 11. We truly have seen the best. Tales have circu-
lated of ordinary citizens joining forces with public servants
in the heroic rescue efforts. Numerous stories have emerged
of heroes who risked their lives to try to save people they
often didn't even know. Many, of course, lost their own lives
in the effort.

On that day of infamy, two young men in Tower One, just
eight stories below where the plane hit, were trying to make
their way down the stairs to safety when they came upon a
woman stranded in her wheelchair on the sixty-eighth floor.
Instead of passing by, they placed her in a special lightweight
chair and carefully carried her down the stairs while smoke
poured into the stairwell and the steel beams began to melt.
Finally they reached the street and got the woman into a waiting ambulance. Minutes later the building began to collapse,
and the men ran for their lives. As they did, they found their
way into a nearby church and fell inside, thankful to be alive.[6]

Ray Downey, New York City's most decorated firefighter, was on the scene at the World Trade Center. After the first plane hit the north tower, he met with the mayor and other fire officials to set up an evacuation plan. And then he went into the north tower to help implement that plan. He was last seen in the lobby of the building just before it collapsed.[7]

The U.S. Department of Defense announced on September 27 that civilian employees of the department killed or injured in the September 11 attack will receive the new Defense of Freedom Medal. Members of the armed services killed or injured at the Pentagon that day will receive the Purple Heart. In the Department of Defense's eyes—and our own—they are all heroes.

President Bush obviously felt this when he made a visit to Washington Hospital Center to visit victims of the attack on the Pentagon. Stopping to encourage one colonel who was badly burned over 50 percent of his body, the president talked and prayed with him. Then he stood at the foot of the victim's bed and saluted. The president held that salute as the officer, with burned and bandaged arms, ever so slowly returned the salute. Normally an officer of lesser rank initiates a salute to one of higher rank. As commander in chief of U.S. Armed Forces, this was President Bush's way of showing honor and respect to the wounded colonel.

After the plane hit the Pentagon, a forty-one-year-old Army health policy officer used her skills as a burn-care and trauma nurse. She set up a triage center where she treated more than seventy-five people, initially with only minimal first aid supplies. She put evacuees to work cutting the clothing off burn victims even before EMT workers arrived.[8]

A Virginia state trooper who helped three workers escape

the Pentagon fire later ended up himself in an intensive care unit with throat burns. "All this hero stuff—I don't want it," he said. "I'm just glad I was there to help."[9]

We'll never know all the stories, but we salute these men and women and the thousands of public servants and volunteers who truly are heroes of our nation and role models for our children. They are an inspiration to us all.

PRAYER

Lord, thank you for the heroes who put their lives at stake to save others—not just one day, but year round. Bless those who are grieving today over a lost hero. Bless those who survived, but are still scared from their harrowing ordeal. Lord, we are grateful for each and every one of them. Amen.

Give Us Hope

———— ✎ ————

Be strong and take heart,
All you who hope in the Lord.

PSALM 31:24

Pastor John H. Gladstone once said, "No human situation is hopeless if God is taken into account—and God is waiting for us to wait on him! He is waiting for us to realize that when we reach the end of our tether, he is there."[10] He was right.

Hope is God's gift to us. It is the calm that tempers the winds of adversity threatening to sink our ship. "To hope," according to *Webster's Dictionary,* means simply "to cherish a desire with expectation of fulfillment." Even though we're surrounded by chaos and havoc, hope is that stirring within our souls that motivates us to survive the present and believe in the future.

When the first plane hit one of the towers of the World Trade Center, thirty-seven-year-old Jun Lee, on the concourse below the WTC complex, knew she had to get out. She was nine months pregnant—now ten days overdue—and wearing flip-flops because of her badly swollen feet. Walking was difficult enough, never mind trying to run.

Thinking, "I'm nine months pregnant. I'm going to die," she fled as fast as she could into the chaos of the street and headed away from the towers. She tired quickly, but had to keep going because there was no place to stop. About ten

blocks away she took refuge in a hotel and called her husband. He later joined her there and they booked a room.
Soon the hotel lost electric power and phone service.

At midnight, Jun Lee began having serious contractions.
Fearing the prospect of a delivery in the dark with no doctor,
the couple struck out, walking through the ash-covered, de-
serted streets to the hospital two miles away. It was a tough,
ninety-minute trek, but they made it. And eight hours later
baby Elizabeth was born.

"I never thought I'd be so happy to see this baby," the
mother said.[11]

The birth of a child is always worth celebrating. But this
baby's entry into the world made headlines. Her story stood
as a remarkable sign of hope in the midst of a time of great
confusion and anguish. As American poet Carl Sandburg
put it, "A baby is God's opinion that the world should go
on." We were all strengthened and encouraged by the hope
this little life gave us.

No matter how difficult life may be, never let circumstances convince you to let go of your hope. Remind yourself
that good things may be lurking right around the corner. Let
your hope grow, not wane. It has the power to steady you.

≫

PRAYER

*Lord, thank you that the hope we have in you is an anchor for
our souls. Help us to cling to you in the midst of our darkness
and find the ray of hope that will lead us to a brighter tomorrow. Amen.*

4

PRAYING FOR OUR NATIONAL LEADERS

I now leave, not knowing when or whether ever I may return, with a task before me greater than that which rested upon Washington. Without the assistance of that Divine Being who ever attended him, I cannot succeed. With that assistance I cannot fail. Trusting in Him who can go with me, and remain with you, and be everywhere for good, let us confidently hope that all will yet be well.

ABRAHAM LINCOLN, IN A FAREWELL ADDRESS IN
SPRINGFIELD, ILLINOIS, FEBRUARY 11, 1861,
BEFORE LEAVING FOR WASHINGTON

Abraham Lincoln, like many presidents who preceded him, clearly recognized the need to call upon God for help in order to fulfill the demanding duties of a national office. So many issues require action, and literally millions of people will be affected by the decisions taken. We depend on God to guide our national leaders as we faithfully pray for them.

Our President and
His Cabinet

———— ✒ ————

I urge, then, first of all, that requests, prayers, intercession and
thanksgiving be made for everyone—for kings and all those in
authority, that we may live peaceful and quiet lives in all godliness and holiness.

1 TIMOTHY 2:1-2

Our president sets the moral tone for our nation. He
encourages us, believes in us, prays for us, and trusts
in the resilience of the American people.

Just listen to the words of encouragement spoken by President George W. Bush at a joint session of Congress, the
night of September 20 following the terrorist attack on our
country:

Tonight, we are a country awakened to danger and
called to defend freedom. Our grief has turned to
anger and anger to resolution . . . Americans are asking, "Why do they [the terrorists] hate us?" They hate
what they see right here in this chamber—a demo-
cratically elected government. Their leaders are self-
appointed. They hate our freedoms: our freedom of
religion, our freedom of speech, our freedom to vote
and assemble and disagree with each other . . . Please
continue praying for the victims of terror and their
families, for those in uniform, and for our great coun-

try. Prayer has comforted us in sorrow and will help strengthen us for the journey ahead . . . Tonight I thank my fellow Americans for what you have already done and for what you will do.

The president expressly thanked members of Congress for their unity and support, then held up the police shield badge that had belonged to George Howard, an officer of the New York Port Authority who died at the World Trade Center while trying to save others. "I'll carry it as a reminder of lives that ended and a task that does not end," he said. "I will not forget the wound to our country and those who inflicted it. I will not yield. I will not rest. I will not relent in waging this struggle for freedom and security. In all that lies before us, may God grant us wisdom, and may he watch over the United States of America."

The president is our chief executive officer, commander in chief of the army, head of state and treaty maker. He formulates foreign policy, drafts legislation, and leads his political party. Almost every decision he makes affects not only our nation but also has worldwide implications.

With the approval of the Senate he appoints members of his Cabinet, who, when key policy decisions are made, give advice to the president. They also make critical decisions affecting the entire nation regarding domestic and foreign issues.

What an awesome responsibility these leaders have. Let us take up the challenge to pray for them.

PRAYER

Lord, please give our president clarity, insight, and wisdom to lead our nation. May he draw upon your strength and guidance for every decision. Give cabinet members wisdom as they advise our president and faithfully fulfill their duties in the best interest of our county. We ask for your mercy, Lord, in all that lies ahead for America. Amen.

Congress

―――――――――― // ――――――――――

For it is God who works in you to will and to act according to
his good purpose.

PHILIPPIANS 2:13

Prayer was a foundation stone in our early American history. Not only did our leaders openly pray, they encouraged the people of this growing nation to pray on numerous occasions.

For instance, on October 18, 1780, the Continental Congress issued a Proclamation for a Day of Public Thanksgiving and Prayer after Benedict Arnold's plot to betray General George Washington and his troops to the British was uncovered. (Likewise, President George W. Bush declared a Day of Prayer and Remembrance three days after our recent national tragedy.)

Our United States Congress, established under the Constitution in 1789, is today composed of two houses: (1) the Senate, with one hundred members, in which each state, regardless of its size, is represented by two senators; and (2) the House of Representatives, with 435 members, to which delegates are elected on the basis of population. Together these bodies are known as the legislative branch, or the lawmakers. Their duties vary from such matters as government printing to general accounting to the national budget. Other agencies are responsible to Congress and the president submits certain types of treaties and nominations to the Senate for approval. At the beginning of each yearly session of Congress the president delivers a State of the Union address describing the legislative program he would like Congress to consider. He later submits an annual budget for their consideration.

Liberals and conservatives. Debates and disagreements. Bipartisan differences often flare up on the floor of Congress. With so many things to consider and vote upon, sometimes reason gives way to highly charged emotions.

With all the responsibility vested in them, it is extremely important that each of us:

- learns the names of the senators and representatives from our state and prays for them, maybe even sends a letter of encouragement once in a while
- prays for wisdom for the entire body of Congress
- prays for them to lay aside personal vendettas and pass laws for the benefit of the nation
- be faithful in voting during elections and ask God for wisdom when we vote

In the wake of our nation's recent tragedy, we saw members of Congress work together across party lines to pass a resolution pledging their support of the president, giving him authority to take whatever measures he deemed necessary. They took this action, even though the president already possessed legal power to act. Since the tragedy, both parties have emphasized unity and gone out of their way to avoid clashes. In this they are worthy of our gratitude . . . and our prayers.

PRAYER

Lord, we ask that those who serve as our representatives in Congress—passing legislation that affects all of us—will make prudent decisions, especially when our nation is in crisis. May they maintain integrity and lead our nation with dignity and righteousness. Amen.

Military Leaders

———— ✔ ————

But with us is the LORD our God to help us and to fight our battles.

2 CHRONICLES 32:8

In an interview with *Christianity Today,* retired general H. Norman Schwarzkopf said that more than competence, *character* is the fundamental attribute of great leaders, including military leaders. He said:

> It's more important than anything else. Competence is important, certainly, but if you had to sacrifice one, you would give up competence before character. In these uncertain days facing our nation, we look to our military leaders. In doing so, we pray that they will be men and women of strong character.[1]

Schwarzkopf feels that leadership in the military is a calling, much like leadership in the church. "It is a belief in serving something other than yourself, serving a higher cause. In our case, it's the cause of duty and honor and country that we are serving."

He said to instill confidence in people facing a fearful situation, a leader needs to acknowledge that he understands the danger, yet still is in command of the situation. "The right attitude is, 'We will face that which is causing our fear and prevail.' "

He also said a good leader needs to impart faith to the

people under his command: faith in him as a leader, faith in the cause, faith in themselves, and ultimately faith in the Lord. "For if the cause is indeed just, he will ultimately prevail."[2]

General Dwight D. Eisenhower, the supreme commander of the Allied Forces during World War II, understood this well. On the night of July 10, 1943, he stood on the shores of Malta observing the armada of three thousand naval ships he had ordered to battle. He saluted his men as they set out for the shores of Sicily, then bowed his head in prayer. Turning to the officer next to him he commented, "There comes a time when you've used your brains, your training, your technical skill, and the die is cast . . . the events are in the hands of God, and there you have to leave them."[3]

Recently I (Quin) sat next to a serviceman on an airplane. I told him how much I appreciated his sacrifice for our country and that I pray for our military. He looked at me in disbelief. No one had ever told him that. But that didn't keep him from replying. "Don't stop praying," he said.

Rank-and-file members of our nation's military need leaders who will instill confidence and who will inspire them to believe in the rightness of their mission. We can pray that God will raise up mighty men and women of honor, character, competence, and courage for such times as these.

❁

PRAYER

Lord, throughout history you have raised up military leaders; they are among your chosen servants. Give them wisdom as they lead, as they make life and death decisions. May your hand of favor be upon them and upon us. For it's in you we trust. Amen.

Transportation Authorities

———————— ✠ ————————

The LORD will watch over your coming and going
Both now and forevermore.

PSALM 121:8

Immediately after the terrorists' attacks, "the skies of America closed," as one *Washington Post* reporter wrote.[4] Airports were shuttered and all flights were canceled. When the airports opened a week later, travelers stayed home in droves. The skies were no longer friendly.

The travel industry has taken a hard hit, just as it did during the 1991 Persian Gulf War. But this time it's different. This time we feel unsafe everywhere, not just in the air. What if our enemies attack our highways? What if they attack our subways? Will trains be next? What about buses? Are our bridges and tunnels and harbors safe?

At the beginning of the twenty-first century, the United States, including Alaska and Hawaii, had 14,572 airports, 22 ports and harbors, 149,129 miles of railways, 3,944,605 miles of highway, and 25,482 miles of navigable inland waterway channels (not including the Great Lakes).[5] Imagine the job of overseeing this vast network.

But God knows each square inch, each drop of water, each speck of concrete. Robert Nelson Spencer penned the following words to be sung as an additional verse to an already beloved hymn, "Eternal Father, Strong to Save," also known as the Navy Hymn:

O Christ, the Lord of hill and plain,
O'er which our traffic runs a-main
By mountain pass or valley low:
Wherever, Lord, Thy brethren go,
Protect them by Thy guarding hand
From every peril on the land.
Before Thy throne we humbly bend;
To us Thy saving grace extend.

Spencer's lyrics reminds us that God is Lord over hill and plain. He watches over our comings and goings, both now and forevermore. He also watches over those who have the responsibility of keeping our highways, waterways, and even our skies safe for travel—from the secretary of transportation to city bus drivers.

As they seek to restore and maintain safety and confidence, we pray God's wisdom and protection for:

- the secretary of transportation as he leads those under him
- armed marshals on airline flights
- pilots, flight attendants, and air traffic controllers
- airport administrators and security personnel
- railroad workers
- city transit workers
- port authority personnel
- highway workers
- truck, taxi, and bus drivers

Americans are newly aware that every time they board a plane, train, or bus, hail a taxi, or ride in a carpool, they are putting their lives into someone else's hands. We've probably taken for granted the blessings of a reliable transportation system. But we now realize as never before that we're dependent upon God to protect us and responsible to pray for those who work hard to make our means of travel safe.

↝

PRAYER

Lord, we feel vulnerable, but you are able to protect us anywhere we may go. We ask that your hand of protection be on us in all our travels and especially on those whom we entrust with our safety. Amen.

Security and
Intelligence Officers

Then Joshua son of Nun secretly sent two spies from Shittim. "Go, look over the land," he said, "especially Jericho."

JOSHUA 2:1

During the Revolutionary War, both the British and American forces communicated information about the opposing force's military strategies through letters, which were sent through spy networks. British spies devised clever means of concealing their messages. They inserted letters into hollow quills of large feathers, sewed them into buttons, even stuffed them into small silver balls the size of rifle bullets.

When British spy Daniel Taylor was captured at New Windsor, he swallowed the silver ball he was carrying. His captors forced him to vomit, but when he did, he retrieved the ball and swallowed it again. Only after an American general threatened to hang him and cut the message out of his stomach did Taylor agree to again regurgitate the ball. Afterwards he was court-martialed and later executed.

In any war, securing victory over one's enemy requires tight security and the use of the most current means of gathering intelligence. In the military, *intelligence* denotes information about the enemy. But gathering such information doesn't come without risk. Those who serve in this area constantly put their lives on the line for the safety of American citizens.

In this war against terrorism we face, let us keep in prayer those who do the dangerous work of intelligence and security. We pray for:

- the attorney general
- the directors of the Central Intelligence Agency (CIA) and their agents
- the Federal Bureau of Investigation (FBI) and their agents
- military personnel who work with cryptography and communication codes
- directors and personnel at the National Security Agency

Pray that:

- God will raise up men and women of loyalty and integrity who will not grow weary in their jobs
- our enemies' secrets will be uncovered and their evil plans thwarted
- God will protect our secrets and expose spies in our own ranks

National security is a matter that the average American has not been overly concerned about, especially since the fall of European communism. Perhaps our economic growth and unprecedented prosperity lulled us into a false sense of security. But all that has changed now. Policies enacted by security and intelligence agencies impact every American. We should give them our support.

PRAYER

Lord, of all our weapons and strategies and means of gathering intelligence, you have given us prayer as the most effective and powerful tool at our disposal. So we pray that you will help us know our enemy. Even more important, help us to know you. For knowing you is the greatest security measure we have. Amen.

5

PRAYING FOR OUR FAMILIES

The family has always been the cornerstone of American society. Our families nurture, preserve, and pass on to each succeeding generation the values we share and cherish, values that are the foundation for our freedoms. In the family we learn our first lessons of God and man, love and discipline, rights and responsibilities, human dignity and human frailty.

RONALD WILSON REAGAN,
IN HIS BOOK *REBIRTH OF AMERICA*

Human history began with a family—Adam and Eve and their sons Cain and Abel. Members of this first household in Scripture had problems getting along with one another, just as members of many modern families do. But God cares deeply about families. He went to great lengths to save Noah's. He continues to care about our families today, and as we pray he can help us resolve the problems we face.

Protection

He who dwells in the shelter of the Most High
Will rest in the shadow of the Almighty.
I will say of the LORD, "He is my refuge and my fortress,
My God, in whom I trust."

PSALM 91:1-2

In the immediate aftermath of the September 11 attacks, phone lines across the country were jammed as family members called to check on one another. Some of the saddest stories to emerge from the tragedy involved the haunting calls by people who were trappd in the highest floors of the World Trade Center towers. Many of them called their spouses to bid farewell when they realized that they were about to perish. In the days that followed, thousands of people in New York posted pictures of their missing loved ones at the Wall of Prayer and on light posts, desperately hoping to reunite their families.

This horrible event reminded us of the importance of family relationships. During a crisis, families come together to find comfort and strength. So in the everyday routine of life, how can we pray for our family? Here are some things we can ask for:

- for peace in our homes
- for godly and loving parents
- for a home filled with God's love
- for healthy relationships among siblings and extended family members

- for a safe and nurturing haven where we can feel accepted just as we are
- for wholesome friendships and godly role models

The growing number of reports of violence in our schools has spawned fear in the hearts of parents as they watch their youngsters grow up in a changing and unstable world. But our response can be proactive. We can pray daily for God's hand of protection to be over our school children, teenagers, and young adults. We can pray for God's wisdom and strength to guide their teachers, coaches, scout leaders, and employers. And we can pray that our children would develop wholesome friends who have a positive influence over them.

All parents are concerned about the protection of their children and we try to take sensible precautions. But what a comfort to know that we can pray for God's protection over them and be assured that he will not leave them!

PRAYER

Lord, I ask for your divine protection over my children and my family members. Keep them alert to danger and help them avoid perilous situations. Protect them from evil companions and help them to cultivate godly friendships. Thank you for all the ways you have already protected them and kept them safe. Watch over them like a mother hen watches over her chicks. Amen.

Blessings for Our Children

———— ✦ ————

We will tell the next generation
The praiseworthy deeds of the LORD,
His power, and the wonders he has done . . .
Then they would put their trust in God
And would not forget his deeds
But would keep his commands.

PSALM 78:4, 7

What do we tell our children and grandchildren today to lift their spirits in spite of the uncertainty of life around them? We can reflect on the good things in life, the blessings God has given us. We can tell them stories about our family—some funny, some more serious—and help them appreciate what is wholesome and right in our lives. We can share our spiritual heritage, telling them about our own journey with God and how they can know and enjoy that too. We can teach them that the Lord is their best friend and that they can always call upon him in times of trouble or fear.

Most of all we can pray for them. Not only for their protection but that they will grow up to be responsible citizens. Here are some Bible-based prayers you can pray for your children:

- that the Lord will deliver them from evil (Matt. 6:13)
- that the Lord will command his angels to guard them in all their ways (Ps. 91:11)
- that they will be taught of the Lord and that their peace will be great (Isa. 54:13)

- that they will choose companions who are wise (Prov. 13:20, 1 Cor. 5:11)
- that they will honor their parents (Eph. 6:1-3)
- that they will fulfill the plans God has for their lives, to give them a hope and a future (Jer. 29:11)
- that they will train themselves to discern good from evil and have a good conscience toward God (Heb. 5:14; 1 Peter 3:21)
- that they will enjoy good health and that all will go well with them, physically and spiritually (3 John 2)
- that they will grow in wisdom and stature and in favor with God and the people their lives touch (Luke 2:52)
- that they, like Daniel, will show "aptitude for every kind of learning," be "well informed, quick to understand, and qualified to serve" (Dan. 1:4)
- that they, like Solomon, will have "wisdom and great insight, and a breadth of understanding as measureless as the sand on the seashore" (1 Kings 4:29)

Supported by our prayers, godly young men and women can accomplish feats they never dreamed possible. God is looking for committed people through whom he can change the world, and our sons and daughters and grandchildren could be the ones he uses. Let's pray they will be blessed and ready.

PRAYER

*T*hank you, Lord, for my children. Indeed they are precious gifts you have given. Help me to be faithful and diligent in praying for them and for the people in their lives who influence them every day. Lord, thank you in advance for hearing me. Amen.

Provision and Blessing

> How blessed is the man who fears the LORD,
> Who greatly delights in His commandments . . .
> The generation of the upright will be blessed.
>
> PSALM 112:1b, 2b

How quickly we get the jitters when analysts say America's economic health is in decline. We focus on the Dow Jones average. We worry about the Federal Reserve's action on interest rates. We anxiously await quarterly announcements from various American industries and the government's economic indicators.

Too often we rely on these indices and listen to the Wall Street analysts, forgetting that it is God who gives us the ability to make wealth (Deut. 8:18). In other words, we must look to God for our provision, especially in times of financial uncertainty, for ultimately, God is our source. He is ever with us, blessing us and providing for us. Indeed, one of the Hebrew names for God is Jehovah-Jireh, "our provider."

There is the story of a farm family who lost everything during a period of recession. When farm prices and the cattle market plunged, Ruth and her husband faced foreclosure, bankruptcy, and selling off their possessions—including the home place and pastureland that had been in their families for generations. She said:

One day, looking at the farm machinery all lined up for the sale, I remembered what a friend had said when their tractor had fallen apart: "Big deal—it's just a piece of steel." I put a sign on the chicken house that read, "There is life after farming." My only recourse was to hold on to my faith in God—that was something they couldn't take away from me.

I do not understand all that has happened to me, or why it has happened. But I do understand that this earth is not my real home. Jesus, my savior, has prepared a place for me. The Lord has proved himself faithful over and over as my provider.[1]

This family might have lost physical possessions, but they didn't lose their faith and today they are happy with the simple things of life. Rather than being discouraged, Ruth clings to these verses, which she calls her "rope of hope":

"For I know the plans I have for you," declares the Lord, "plans to prosper you and not to harm you, plans to give you hope and a future. Then you will call upon me and come and pray to me, and I will listen to you . . . I will bring you back from captivity." (Jer. 29:11–12, 14a)

As you pray for blessing and provision for your family and friends, allow the words of Robert Louis Stevenson to give you perspective: "The best things are nearest: breath in your nostrils, light in your eyes, flowers at your feet, duties at your hand, the path of God just before you."

PRAYER

Lord, keep me mindful that you are my source, my provider. I trust you to give me the power to find a job and meet my responsibilities. Help me to be a good steward of all you have provided. I am so thankful for every blessing. Amen.

Forgiveness and Reconciliation

---~---

Do not judge, and you will not be judged. Do not condemn, and
you will not be condemned. Forgive, and you will be forgiven.

LUKE 6:37

Forgiveness is usually the first step toward reconciliation
in families that have been wounded by division or misunderstanding. Too often we hold onto our "right to be
right"—no matter what! Not only are we hurt by this stance,
but other family members may take up the offense on our
behalf. They can easily be pulled into our squabble—even if
the dispute is over some petty matter.

To forgive has several shades of meaning:

- to absolve from payment of a debt
- to excuse from a fault or an offense
- to give up the wish to punish or get even
- to bestow a favor unconditionally
- to release, set at liberty, unchain

I (Quin) once heard a pastor say, "To forgive is like the ac-
quittal of a defendant—clearing him even if he's guilty and
dealing with him as though innocent." Forgiveness is an act
of the will, not an emotion. It's a choice, a decision, an act of
love. Our part is to forgive, even if we feel no emotion about
it. God's part is to heal.

I (Quin) had harbored a deep-seated resentment against

my dad for abandoning my mother with four children when I was young. I was married with three children the night I knelt in a little church in Florida and chose to forgive him. I began writing letters to reestablish a relationship with him. Five years later, for the first time since I had married, he came alone to see me.

"How could you love me after all I've done?" he asked on the third day of his visit. I think he already knew: I could love again because I had long before chosen to forgive him.

I personally know how wonderful it is when forgiveness is extended, grudges laid aside, and fellowship restored. I also know people who have forgiven, but for whom reconciliation has not happened. But the point is the one who forgives is no longer in bondage. When we forgive it doesn't mean our aggressor gets off free, but it does mean we are free, unchained. When we don't forgive, we bind ourselves to that person or situation, and to the pain, emotional hurt, and consequences it brings. When we forgive, we are set free.

Jesus makes it clear that if we want his forgiveness, we must be willing to forgive. When we make the choice to obey him, we receive his strength to carry through. The benefit we receive is worth the struggle to forgive those who wrong us, no matter how painful the offense.

PRAYER

Father, forgive us for the grievances we hold against one another. Help us to forgive to the degree you desire and expect—we need your strength to do it. We pray for reconciliation in our families, churches, and communities. Lord, let it start with me. Amen.

Strength and Courage

———————— ✐ ————————

Don't be afraid . . . Remember the Lord, who is great and awesome, and fight for your brothers, your sons and your daughters, your wives and your homes.

NEHEMIAH 4:14

As you attempt to maintain strength and courage by praying for your family, you can draw hope from the story of Nehemiah in the Old Testament. He and his band of Jewish refugees set out to rebuild the broken-down walls of Jerusalem, but they met with enormous opposition. Their enemies tried to frighten them, discourage them, or distract them enough to stop the work. But Nehemiah and his people refused to give up.

In praying daily for your family, thoughts of giving in may assault your mind. This is the battlefield where our enemy so often attacks. But God can strengthen us and give us courage to keep praying. It's always too soon to quit!

Before beginning his task, Nehemiah asked God's forgiveness for the disobedience of his ancestors: "I confess the sins we Israelites, including myself and my father's house, have committed against you." (Neh. 1:6). Then Nehemiah reminded the Lord that these were God's own people living in Jerusalem, and that the walls needed rebuilding to prevent their enemies from having free access to their homes: "O Lord, let your ear be attentive to the prayer of this your servant . . . Give your servant success today." (Neh. 1:11).

And then, in the face of ridicule, Nehemiah had faith:

"The God of heaven will give us success. We his servants will start rebuilding, but as for you, you have no share in Jerusalem or any claim or historic right to it" (Neh. 2:20).

Nehemiah posted a guard day and night to meet the enemy's threats. He organized the people to work in shifts. Family members worked together until the wall was rebuilt without a gap in just fifty-two days. When Nehemiah's enemies heard about it, "all the surrounding nations were afraid and lost their self-confidence, because they realized that this work had been done with the help of our God" (Neh. 6:16).

Nehemiah later led the people in a grand celebration as they listened to the reading of the word of God. They wept, sang, bowed down, and celebrated as their leader reminded them, "The joy of the Lord is your strength" (Neh. 8:10).

Like Nehemiah, we too face formidable enemies, both physical and nonphysical. They will look for areas of vulnerability in our families. To overcome them will require strength, courage, and persistence. But if we do not give up the battle, we will be victorious. The Lord has promised us so.

PRAYER

Lord, keep me steadfast and courageous as I remain faithful to pray for my family. Help me to trust you, so that no matter what I see happening in the natural realm, I won't be overwhelmed. I know you are with us. May the joy of the Lord always be my strength. Amen.

6

PRAYING FOR OUR STATE AND COMMUNITY LEADERS

I am only one, but I am one. I cannot do everything, but I can do something. What I can do, I should do and, with the help of God, I will do!

EVERETT HALE, CHAPLAIN OF THE UNITED STATES SENATE AND GRANDNEPHEW OF NATHAN HALE, THE REVOLUTIONARY PATRIOT EXECUTED BY THE BRITISH AFTER STATING, "I ONLY REGRET THAT I HAVE BUT ONE LIFE TO LOSE FOR MY COUNTRY"

Just one person diligently carrying out his or her duty can impact the safety and security of an entire community. When many work together, the beneficial result is even greater. Governors, legislators, mayors, council members, police officers, firefighters, school administrators, and teachers—they all influence our states, cities, and towns for good or for ill. They need our prayers.

Governor and State Legislators

———— ✌ ————

For he is God's servant to do you good.

ROMANS 13:4

On April 19, 1995, a truck loaded with explosives blew up in front of the Alfred P. Murrah Federal Building in downtown Oklahoma City. We admired Oklahoma Governor Frank Keating for the way he led his state's rescue and recovery operations in the aftermath of that tragedy. Keating and his wife, Cathy, took the lead in creating a six-million-dollar college scholarship fund for children who were injured or had lost parents in the bombing. In recognition, they were awarded the William Booth Award by the Salvation Army.

As governor, Keating set goals for the state to reduce divorces, out-of-wedlock births, substance abuse, and child abuse. He and Cathy organized a statewide initiative to strengthen marriages, using government resources, community, and faith-based groups.

American statesman Senator Henry Clay might have been talking of Governor Keating when he said, "Government is a trust, and the officers of the government are trustees; and both the trust and the trustees are created for the benefit of the people."

The apostle Paul was writing to Christians living in

Rome—a city governed mostly by pagans—when he said, "There is no [governing] authority except that which God has established" (Rom. 13:1). What he was saying was that regardless of political party affiliation or even level of competence, every state governor or member of the state legislature is allowed by God to be in his or her position—even the ones we don't like. These were strong words, considering the political situation of that day. As one commentator says, "Even the possibility of a persecuting state did not shake Paul's conviction that civil government is ordained by God."[1]

Of course we hope all our state leaders will be godly men and women, but that's not always the case. Regardless, all are under God's authority, used for his divine purposes, and need our prayers.

We don't know what the future will bring. Natural disasters and senseless, man-initiated calamities occur frequently and our governors are called upon to guide, direct, comfort, protect, and lead. They need cool heads and strength beyond their abilities.

New York Governor George Pataki, in the aftermath of the twin towers disaster, put aside any misunderstanding with his former adversary, Mayor Rudy Giuliani, to help lead New Yorkers through their darkest hour. Their show of solidarity in the interest of helping the victims provided an example for others to follow.

So as we focus our prayers for our state leaders, let us ask the Lord for:

- personal integrity—we pray that our leaders will conduct themselves ethically, both in their public and private life

- faith-friendly legislation—we pray for legislators to draft legislation that upholds biblical values and principles that preserve the sanctity of life for individuals, faith groups, and families
- wise stewardship of tax revenues and resources

PRAYER

Lord, strengthen our governor. Let our state leaders understand their roles as trustees. May they put people above politics and you above all else. Amen.

Mayor, City Council, and Business Leaders

—— 〰 ——

Who then is the faithful and wise manager?

LUKE 12:42

According to the *U.S. Mayor* newspaper, shortly after the September 11 terrorist attacks, the U.S. Conference of Mayors surveyed mayors of American cities with populations greater than thirty thousand. They were asked what they and their cities had done in response to the catastrophic events. Of the more than two hundred mayors who answered the survey, most responded to the attacks by first calming the citizens, then urging them to pray. Next came encouragement to donate blood and money.[2] Their first concern was to bring the communities together—to work together and seek altruistic ways to work out their grief and desire to do something constructive.

An example of this leadership is Mayor Joseph Doria Jr., who opened the city of Bayonne, N.J., to those escaping nearby Manhattan. Under his leadership, local stores stayed open and were used as shelters. Local residents opened their homes to New Yorkers needing a place to stay.

Some people may feel the role of mayor or city council member is rather insignificant. But this is not so—especially during a crisis. On September 23, 2001, Mayor Rudolph Giuliani and religious leaders gathered with more than twenty thousand people in New York's Yankee Stadium to pray and remember those who died. "You have to concentrate on the good things," the mayor said. "Life presents as many opportunities for happiness as it does for tragedy."

Since the business community is a vital part of our lives, we also need to pray that employers and managers will find creative ways to keep their businesses solvent and provide employment for local residents. "Our country's wealth is not contained in glass and steel," said President Bush in his speech to Congress and the nation after the attacks. "It is found in the skill and hard work and entrepreneurship of our people."

No job or position is too small in God's eyes, either in the business community and the world of commerce, or in local government. Businessmen and local officials are an important part of our cities, and they need our prayers. Their jobs offer great opportunities to affect people where they live. Mayors and council members deal with many mundane matters, but they also decide about speed bumps and traffic lights that may save the life of a teenage driver. That's *big*.

As citizens, we can encourage our local government officials by:

- writing letters to the local paper publicly commending their good decisions
- attending public meetings to show support for them
- refraining from name-calling and back-biting
- praying for them

PRAYER

Lord, help our local officials and business leaders to be faithful in their duties and to unite our community. Give them wisdom to keep our city clean and safe and prosperous. May your will be done through them, that their efforts, large and small, will bring honor to you. Amen.

Police Officers

Blessed are the peacemakers.

MATTHEW 5:9

According to Steve Lee, police chaplain and founder of Peace Officer Ministries, the average citizen sees police officers as a badge and a gun, not as ordinary people doing a difficult job. But as ordinary people, they need our encouragement and prayers.

Lee told *Christianity Today* that police officers live in the realm of the law. Their view of God is legally based, with clearly defined ideas of right and wrong, good and bad. Typically, a police officer feels pressure to be moral and legally responsible. However, human beings don't have the capacity to endure such perfectionism, he said. As a result, police officers are at a high risk for divorce, suicide, and alcoholism. Lee said the divorce rate among officers is higher than 80 percent and that they are "three to four times as likely to commit suicide than be killed in the line of duty."[3]

Police officers need the grace of God, especially in their appointed roles as ministers of peace. They are the ones called upon and placed on the front lines of disorder and dispute, chaos and terror. Unfortunately some, as a defense mechanism, harden their hearts to the pain and suffering and human depravity they're subjected to on a daily basis.

Lee feels that law enforcement is not like other professions. "With the police, there's an emotional and spiritual distance from people that needs to be bridged," he said.[4]

Peace Officer Ministries in Colorado Springs offers the following guidelines for praying for police officers:

Pray for the four foundational needs of law enforcement officers:

- physical protection
- emotional protection (depression, anger, suicide, alcoholism, etc.)
- relational protection (divorce, abuse, promiscuity)
- spiritual protection (disillusionment, abandonment of beliefs, cynicism, rejection of the gospel)

Also pray:

- that officers will be able to fulfill their call from God (Rom. 13) and uphold justice
- that faithful officers will be protected from frivolous lawsuits and unfair or biased administrative action based on their religious beliefs
- for unity and a sense of camaraderie within the various departments and divisions of officers
- for the families of law enforcement officers, who also share a greater burden of emotional and relational problems

After the Oklahoma City bombing, the culprit was apprehended when a police officer made a routine stop for a traffic violation. This is only one of the many incidents in a long list of ways our law enforcement officers guard us daily. May we ever be thankful for their vigilance.

PRAYER

Lord, *you have established all governing authorities in our communities, including police officers who protect and defend our peace. We bless them and thank you for them. We pray that you will watch over them and bring your peace to their souls. Amen.*

Firefighters

———— ⟋⟋ ————

Greater love has no one than this, that he lay down his life for his friends.

JOHN 15:13

By now most of us have heard the story. After the attack on the twin towers of the World Trade Center, as people rushed away from the buildings, firefighters and rescue workers rushed into them to their peril. In all, an estimated 340 New York City firefighters perished in the inferno and the collapse of the towers.

One of the most poignant moments in the aftermath was the scene of rescue firefighters finding the body of one of their own. They carefully carried him out of the rubble, gently laid his body on a stretcher, and draped an American flag over him. Then they all stood at attention as the fire chaplain prayed. During the continuing rescue efforts throughout the weeks following September 11, this scene was played out many times over as firefighters found the bodies of their fallen comrades.

Among the hundreds of firefighters who lost their lives, Squad 41 lost six men, including firefighter Tom Foley, the previous year's recipient of the "Bravest" award.

On August 30, 1999, a scaffold outside a Manhattan highrise collapsed and left a workman dangling. Squad 41 was called. When they discovered their aerial ladder couldn't reach the man, Foley volunteered to be lowered down by a hoist from the roof to where the man dangled from the twelfth story of the seventeen-story building. Using his sheer strength, he held onto the man. Then, straddling the rails of the fire truck's aerial ladder, he carried the man over to the ladder and then down to safety. This selfless feat earned him one of Squad 41's highest honors.[5]

In metropolitan cities and small towns across the nation, brave men and women risk their lives daily in service to their communities. They've always been our heroes. It took a national disaster to remind us afresh of their service and sacrifice. These selfless servants, many of whom serve as volunteers, need our encouragement and prayers. We can:

- pray for their safety
- pray for their families, their marriages
- pray for their physical strength and emotional health
- pray that each firefighter in our community will learn to rely on God.

~

PRAYER

Lord, it takes a special person to willingly risk his life for another, especially for a stranger. Thank you for each of our nation's firefighters and especially those in my community. Protect them as they protect me and my family and neighbors. Show me practical ways to reach out to them with the grace of the gospel and the love of God. Amen.

7

Praying for Our Spiritual Leaders and Churches

I sought for the key to the greatness and genius of America in her harbors . . . in her fertile fields and boundless forests; in her rich mines and vast world commerce; in her public school system and institutions of learning. I sought for it in her democratic Congress and in her matchless Constitution.

Not until I went to the churches of America and heard her pulpits flame with righteousness did I understand the secret of her genius and power. America is great because America is good, and if America ever ceases to be good, America will cease to be great.

ALEXIS DE TOCQUEVILLLE, THE FRENCH HISTORIAN WHO CAME TO AMERICA IN 1831 TO OBSERVE THE AMERICAN PEOPLE AND THEIR INSTITUTIONS

Church leaders are in the forefront in America's communities—leading and teaching their people how to exhibit God's heart of compassion, mercy, and grace. They call us to acknowledge our responsibility to share the good news, feed the hungry, clothe the poor. We must fulfill our responsibility to pray for them and their families.

Humility and Repentance

If my people, who are called by my name, will humble them-selves and pray and seek my face and turn from their wicked ways, then will I hear from heaven and will forgive their sin and will heal their land.

2 CHRONICLES 7:14

In the above Scripture, God appeared to Solomon and said he had heard his prayer. But he also emphasized the importance of repentance—a crucial key for a nation hoping to enjoy God's favor. Our spiritual leaders carry the respon-sibility to lead their congregations in hearing God's heart-beat for them and for their nation, including corporate repentance.

Pastor Dutch Sheets recalls his experience at a youth prayer gathering in Washington, D.C., that he attended with his teenage daughters and four hundred thousand others:

At one point in the day, as I was in a time of extreme re-pentance for the sins of my generation against the younger generation, I began to feel the deep pain of God regarding these sins. As I repented over . . . things we have done to or passed to their generation, I thought at one point my heart was going to break . . . I was feeling their pain, the Father's broken heart, and my generation's shame . . . This was the pain of inter-cession.[1]

Soon after the terrorists hit, Pastor Sheets told his congregation: "Our message must be one of carefully balanced grace and truth. God's desire is always to forgive and redeem . . . to turn us from our sin, not destroy us for it. He is 'slow to anger and abundant in lovingkindness' (Psalm 86:15 NASB)."

He then shared that we should:

- pray that the church will see a need for humility and repentance
- pray that the church will be able to respond to this crisis with great wisdom
- ask for a turning of our nation back to God and believe God can do so
- ask for God's mercy to triumph (James 2:13)
- pray for comfort in our nation, but that it would be accompanied with a true recognition of our great spiritual need
- pray that President Bush and other government leaders will move with great wisdom and make sound decisions
- forgive those who have wronged us, yet pray for justice (not revenge) to evildoers (Matt. 7:1, Luke 6:37, Rom. 13:4)[2]

When God spoke to Solomon, he said, "If my people . . . will humble themselves and pray" (2 Chron. 7:14). It seems clear he expects his people to repent on behalf of the nation, not just for their own sins. This requires deep and sometimes painful humility. But it is worth it to know God will reward our repentance with his grace—both for us personally and for the nation.

PRAYER

Most merciful God, we confess that we have sinned against you in thought, word and deed, by what we have done, and by what we have left undone. We have not loved you with our whole heart; we have not loved our neighbors as ourselves. We are truly sorry and we humbly repent. For the sake of your Son Jesus Christ, have mercy on us and forgive us that we may delight in your will and walk in your ways, to the glory of your Name. Amen.[3]

Unity and Vision

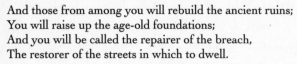

And those from among you will rebuild the ancient ruins;
You will raise up the age-old foundations;
And you will be called the repairer of the breach,
The restorer of the streets in which to dwell.

ISAIAH 58:12

The church has an opportunity as never before to move with a spirit of unity—both in ministering to its own people and in reaching out to those who are seeking God at a new depth. The attack on America has drawn many people to our churches.

"If you had asked me last week if we had a praying church, I'd have said 'No,'" one woman in California remarked. "But after the attack, now I can say, 'Yes.' People flocked to church to pray this week."

Immediately after the towers collapsed, pastors at the Brooklyn Tabernacle opened the church and people began coming in to pray. With New York City's transit system shut down and bridges closed, those who escaped the danger zone were forced to walk. Hundreds of people—covered with dust and ashes—walked across the Brooklyn Bridge from Manhattan and stopped at the church.

"We set up stations to provide drinking water for those who came," said a staff member. "We prayed with some of them, and gave some washcloths so they could clean up—they were so dirty."

In Oregon, a church kept its doors open for prayer around the clock. A man driving in the neighborhood felt compelled to stop and go in. "Even though I grew up in this church, I haven't been to church for more than eighteen years," he told one of the volunteer workers. "When I drove by tonight I just had to stop."[4]

"This is the re-United States of America," said a Boston dockworker as he hugged a flagpole at an interfaith vigil of prayer and solidarity outside Boston's city hall.[5]

Ministry leaders across the country have called for prayer, joining their voices to President Bush's when in his address to Congress and the nation he emphasized the importance of prayer and quoted from the Twenty-Third Psalm. Americans are displaying a renewed interest in God in the midst of their shock and grief. Congregations are ministering to the poor, hungry, and hurting people in their communities and responding to relief efforts in cities most affected by the disasters. They are providing counseling to those who grieve and giving sacrificially to those needing blood and finances.

May those who lead us teach us how to be restorers of the streets in which we live and rebuilders of the foundation of prayer. May all of us hunger to know God better and find his will and his way for us and our families.

PRAYER

God, we ask for unity among your people, especially your spiritual leaders. Help us all to draw closer to one another as we reach out in love to a hurting nation and world. We want to be your hands extended to those in need. Amen.

Speaking the Truth in Love

———— 〰 ————

Join with others in following my example, brothers, and take
note of those who live according to the pattern we gave you.

PHILIPPIANS 3:17

Since the founding of our nation, pastors and spiritual
leaders have had an impact on their communities. They
have stood for truth . . . taken ridicule . . . been misunderstood. But they have left their contribution to the heritage
and well-being of our country.

After colonists landed in Virginia in April 1607, their first
act was to erect a large wooden cross and hold a prayer meeting. Reverend Robert Hunt conducted the service to thank
God for bringing them to this new land. He provided moral
leadership for this nucleus of the first permanent settlement
later known as Jamestown. "He endured every privation, yet
none ever heard him repine," someone said at his funeral.

The townspeople in a little village in France—at great
personal risk—hid their Jewish friends from the Nazis during World War II. Years later when a man investigated the
story, he learned why. As the village pastor preached Sunday
after Sunday, he taught biblical principles about loving your
neighbor as yourself. When German troops invaded, the
townspeople were prepared. One elderly woman said, "Pastor always taught us there comes a time in every life when a
person is asked to do something for Jesus. When our time
came, we knew what to do."[6]

Now, fast-forward to September 11, 2001, New York City. The attack on the World Trade Center drew hundreds of firefighters and police to the scene to help in rescue efforts. But as they began climbing the building's stairwells, the structure collapsed, killing hundreds of New York's finest public servants. Among the dead was the Reverend Mychal Judge, a priest and chaplain for the New York Fire Department who was administering last rites to a fallen fireman when he too was hit by falling debris. At his funeral service, mourners packed the church to honor their "fearless priest."[7]

Whether they lead us by word or example, our spiritual leaders deserve our support. How about a phone call, letter, or e-mail message to let them know you appreciate them?

PRAYER

Lord, thank you for those who have made an impact on our communities with their devotion to you. May we follow their examples in our individual lives and be faithful to pray for them. Amen.

Thanksgiving for Those Who Lead

With this in mind, be alert and always keep on praying for all the saints. Pray also for me, that whenever I open my mouth, words may be given me so that I will fearlessly make known the mystery of the gospel.

EPHESIANS 6:18-19

On September 14, 2001, spiritual leaders of all faiths across America opened their places of worship and led their constituents to participate in the National Day of Prayer and Remembrance. They helped bring emotional stability to our communities as we grieved with those who suffered such terrible losses.

Have you considered praying for the spiritual leaders of your city? They identify with our hurts as well as our joys. They bring comfort and solace when calamity shatters the community. They stand faithfully in prayer on behalf of their constituents. They carry heavy responsibilities, and they need our prayer support.

When my (Quin) congregation committed to pray regularly and specifically for our pastor, it made a difference. He began to explain the Word of God with greater depth and insight. He delivered his messages of hope with boldness and a deeper compassion. He began reaching out to other pastors in the community in an effort to bring unity. He got involved in our newly launched inner-city ministry to the homeless and poor.

Just this week, when I attended the funeral of a twenty-year-old killed in an accident, I watched a pastor weep with his arms about the family, sharing their loss. Yet, more important, I heard the words of encouragement he offered from Scripture, assuring us that this young man had gone on to heaven. His job was to counsel and to minister, and he did so selflessly and thoroughly.

Our ministers join couples in holy matrimony and help us dedicate our babies to God. They counsel the depressed, visit the sick, and officiate at services for those who die. They make speeches, attend committee meetings, and oversee countless details to keep the church doors open. Those with spouses and children attempt to be good mates and parents while also meeting the demands of their ministry.

But because they, too, are human, they daily face some of the same problems and sorrows that we face. Our pastors are there when we need them to encourage, comfort, and cheer us on. How they need our prayer support and our encouragement! Let's stop to remember them in prayer.

PRAYER

Lord, thank you for the pastors who intercede in prayer for our needs and concerns. Give them wisdom beyond their experience for the tasks they daily face. Meet their spiritual, physical, and emotional needs. Bless them and their families with your love. Amen

8

PRAYING FOR OUR FRIENDS, NEIGHBORS, AND COWORKERS

JOHN WESLEY'S RULE

Do all the good you can,
By all the means you can,
In all the ways you can,
In all the places you can,
At all the times you can,
To all the people you can,
As long as ever you can.

JOHN WESLEY, FOUNDER OF
THE METHODIST CHURCH

John Wesley, who is recognized as one of the greatest evangelists of the eighteenth century, wrote in his journal in 1739, "I look upon the world as my parish." In considering our own responsibilities to others, we could think of the world as a series of concentric circles. We're in the center, surrounded by immediate and extended family members, then people in our neighborhoods and cities, counties and states, then our country, then the nations of the world. Let each of us ask the Lord to help us to be an influence for godliness at all these levels.

Comfort Those
in Difficulty

―――――― ✦ ――――――

Encourage the exhausted, and strengthen the feeble. Say to those with anxious heart, "Take courage, fear not."

ISAIAH 35:3,4a (NASB)

A re you sometimes at a loss for ways to comfort a neighbor or coworker who is struggling? The best way is simply to be there to encourage, comfort, or help in practical ways. We live in a world networked together unlike any other time in history. Reaching out keeps us from becoming too introspective and self-serving.

Thousands of Americans responded to the wounded and bereaved in the aftermath of the September 11 attack on America—sending money, giving blood, helping in rescue efforts, saying prayers, lighting candles, and for the most part reaching out to unknown strangers. One reporter covered the news from Ground Zero in New York almost nonstop for the first eleven days after the World Trade Center disaster. When interviewed himself, he said:

Obviously all of this [donated goods, services, money] helps, but my suggestion is that everyone who wants to help should try a little bit harder to be kinder to the people around them, to help out a neighbor or friend or stranger in need, to be a bit more positive in everything they do. People always pull together in times of crisis, then that seems to slip away. Maybe we should be all the more focused on pulling together all the time now.[1]

Americans did reach out with a renewed spirit of togetherness. In Atlanta people took stranded passengers into their homes when all airline flights were grounded. In New York, hotel guests shared their rooms with strangers. They offered meals and showers to people who were covered with dust from the collapsed towers. Millions lit candles at vigils that first Friday night—showing solidarity and honoring those who had died in the attack. The tragedy brought people together in a way that prosperity never could.

Thousands who lost their jobs after the attacks are suffering financial setbacks and now need comforting. We can pray for them personally and for our nation's business climate to improve so that people can find jobs. Other thousands lost loved ones—husbands, wives, mothers, fathers, daughters, sons. We can pray for them, too, that they find their way through the grieving process.

As the initial shock of the tragedy diminishes we will think of other ways to keep supporting and comforting the hurting. Here, in the words of some recipients of kindness, are ideas for ways to offer encouragement:

- "When my husband lost his job, someone left groceries on our doorstep."
- "After we lost our baby, a friend gave us a lovely rose-bush. Each spring its delicate scarlet roses bring immense comfort year after year."
- "When my son went to prison, a close friend came and sat with me and let me talk and cry."

- "I have a friend who always seems to know when I'm going through a hard time. She either sends a card or calls me just to say she's praying for me."[2]

These may not seem like big ways to offer comfort, but the beneficiaries of these kindnesses think otherwise. If you yourself stop to remember, you've most likely at least once had a friend or stranger do something for you when you needed help and encouragement. It was probably a small act of kindness. But the thoughtfulness and expenditure of time the person put into it made the act memorable and significant. You don't have to do something big. Just do something from your heart.

≫

PRAYER

Father, thank you for those who have touched my life when I needed comfort. Forgive me for being so focused on my own problems that I've been less concerned about others. Help me to be sensitive to reaching others in practical ways and showing them your love. Amen.

Guide Our Youth

———— ❧ ————

> Don't let anyone look down on you because you are young, but set an example for the believers in speech, in life, in love, in faith and in purity.
>
> 1 TIMOTHY 4:12

A teenage girl had trouble sleeping after watching the September 11 events on television with her parents—her dad is a commercial pilot and her mother a flight attendant. Several nights later, however, she told them, "Mom and Dad, one good thing may come out of this. A lot of people who feel lost and alone right now will turn to the church and as a result will be led to the Lord."[3]

This young woman is not alone in her thinking. A groundswell of renewal seems to be sweeping across the youth of America. For instance, the See You at the Pole event on September 19, 2001, drew three million teenagers, children, and collegians who met around their flagpoles before school to pray for this nation. The theme, "Desperate for God," was based on Psalm 84:2. Several schools had one thousand or more participants.[4]

Another youth prayer movement was launched in September 2000 when some four hundred thousand youth, children, and parents gathered for "The Call, D.C." at the Washington mall to fast and pray for God to once again visit our nation. "The Call, New England " was held in Boston just eleven days after the terrorist attack on America with some thirty thousand youth and their leaders attending. A fifteen-year-old who was at both events said, "The New England gathering impacted me more, perhaps because our nation had been attacked and we were crying out for God to bring revival."[5]

We also saw an outpouring of youth turning to God after the deadly massacre of twelve students and one teacher at Columbine High School in Littleton, Colorado, on April 20, 1999, when two classmates gunned them down. One of those, Rachel Scott, left a diary recording her prayers and thoughts. Just before she died her killer asked if she believed in God. "You know I do," Rachel replied.[6]

Rachel's funeral service was broadcast uninterrupted on CNN television news. Reports came in that many young people committed their lives to the Lord as they watched the telecast. Her pastor said she reached more through her funeral than she could have reached in her lifetime.[7]

We adults can prepare our children for their destiny in God by teaching them to talk to him when they are small. We can model a lifestyle of prayer, give them prayer tools such as books or videos, share our values and heritage both orally and in written form. Only God knows what will happen if we pray for our youth and model an example of a faith worthy of following.

PRAYER

Lord, I thank you that I see among many young people today a hunger to know you better and a desire to use their gifts for godly purposes. Lord, protect them from evil and direct them in your paths. Amen.

Help Me Share Your Love

"Which of these three do you think was a neighbor to the man who fell into the hands of robbers?"[Jesus asked]. The expert in the law replied, "The one who had mercy on him." Jesus told him, "Go and do likewise."

LUKE 10:36–37

The Parable of the Good Samaritan is a story Jesus told in answer to a religious expert's taunting question, "Who is my neighbor?" The story goes that a Jewish man traveling from Jerusalem to Jericho was attacked by robbers who stripped off his clothes, beat him, and left him half dead by the roadside. Two religious authorities, a priest and a Levite, were traveling the same road. But on seeing the wounded man, each crossed over to the other side.

A third traveler, a Samaritan, saw the man's condition and was filled with compassion. He cleaned his wounds, put the stranger on his own donkey, then took him to the nearest inn, where he looked after him through the night. The next day he paid the innkeeper to watch over the wounded man until he recovered and could return home.

Jesus ended by asking, "Which of these was the true neighbor?" The answer of course is the Samaritan.

Jesus knew that in those days a Jewish man wouldn't interact with a Samaritan. The Samaritans were a mixed race of people who practiced what the Jews considered to be a polluted form of worship. But by telling this story, Jesus illustrated that we shouldn't allow our religion or prejudices to prevent us from reaching out to help someone in need.

Several years ago one young pastor, Carl, and his wife, Angie, went to a derelict, multiracial area of their city and asked God to show them and their small congregation creative ways to reach the people there. They rented a building and began having worship services. Members began walking in twos or threes up and down streets in the neighborhood as they prayed for God's peace and blessings over the families.

The congregation have continued to reach out to the locals. At Christmas they take homemade cookies to every family in the small neighborhood, sing Christmas carols, and tell them, "We want you to know we're praying for you." People in the area have responded by coming to the church for free food and clothing.

"We see barriers down, and people speaking to one another and to us," Angie has said. Prayer and practical outreach are making a difference.[8]

At a time when some Americans are expressing hatred toward Arabs or Muslims, we need to be willing to express love toward those of a different race or religion. As we encounter instances of harassment or hatred toward any ethnic or religious groups in our communities, we need to remember the Good Samaritan. Jesus said we should "Go and do likewise" in following his example. How else can these people come to know that ours is a God of love, not of hate?

PRAYER

Lord, help us to not be prejudiced against people of a different race or religion, but instead to be a Good Samaritan to those we have the capacity to assist. Give us creative ways to express your love to others during these troubled times. Amen.

9

PRAYING FOR OUR ENEMIES

I wish to make an earnest call to everyone that we work together to build a world without violence, a world that loves life, and grows in justice and solidarity . . . May people everywhere, strengthened by divine wisdom, work for a civilization of love, in which there is no room for hatred, discrimination or violence.

With all my heart, I beg God to keep the world in peace. Amen.

POPE JOHN PAUL II, IN HIS PRAYER FOR PEACE, SEPTEMBER 23, 2001, ASTANA, KAZAKHSTAN

When our enemies inflict harm upon us, it's only human nature for us to seek retaliation and strike back. But Jesus taught us, "Love your enemies, do good to those who hate you, bless those who curse you, pray for those who mistreat you" (Luke 6:27–28). Our government officials bear the responsibility of dealing with aggressors and protecting our nation's citizens, and we are responsible to pray for them. But on a personal level, God calls upon us to forgive these enemies and to pray for them as well.

Restrain Their Wrath

If the LORD had not been on our side when men attacked us,
When their anger flared against us,
They would have swallowed us up alive.

PSALM 124:2-3

As horrible as the assault against America was on that terrible Tuesday in September, we learned in the following days that circumstances could have been worse. Much worse. One plane heading for a target in our nation's capital was diverted when several passengers overpowered the terrorists, causing the plane to crash near an empty strip mine. Everyone on board perished, but there were no fatalities on the ground.

While we mourn the loss of thousands of innocent lives in Washington, D.C., Pennsylvania, and New York, we also give thanks to God for every life that was spared. At the same time, we can pray that God will restrain the wrath of our enemies and foil their attempts at further harm.

God has created a universe within which an infinite variety of human actions can take place, whether motivated by love or hate, humility or pride. He created us with the power of choice. And this allows for the possibility of terrible evil brought about by man's inhumanity to man. Even so, God's grace is able to change the aggressor into an ally, as we have seen happen before in our nation's history.

The day after the terrorist attacks, members of a church near Tokyo, Japan, gathered to pray for America. A missionary who observed the scene was struck by the fact that fifty-seven years ago, the Japanese, not the Taliban, were America's sworn enemies. During the course of World War II, the Japanese army killed tens of thousands of innocent people throughout China, Korea, and the Philippines, and also persecuted Christians in Japan. But as awful as the Second World War was, our enemies were eventually defeated and their wrath restrained.

Now, many years later, Japanese believers united their hearts in prayer for America. Annual surveys repeatedly bear out the general goodwill that exists between Japan and America, indicating that the people who hated us half a century ago now name America as the country they most trust and respect.

Today it is hard to imagine such a thing in Afghanistan, Iraq, Iran, or northern Sudan. And it's almost unthinkable that the Taliban or the terrorists might one day abandon their hateful attitudes and replace them with God's love. But what better way to restrain their wrath than to pray that God will subdue their anger by drawing them to himself? With God all things are possible. So let's pray, not for what seems possible to us, but for all the things that are possible for God.

PRAYER

Lord, you see the death and destruction perpetrated against us by radical zealots who show no regard for human life. We cannot comprehend what motivates suicide terrorists to inflict such suffering on others. We can ask only that you restrain their wrath and frustrate their destructive plans by whatever means you choose. Draw them to you and fill them with your love. Do the things, Lord, that only you can do. Amen.

Reveal Your Truth

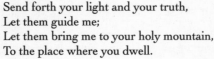

Send forth your light and your truth,
Let them guide me;
Let them bring me to your holy mountain,
To the place where you dwell.

PSALM 43:3

One of America's greatest adversaries in World War II was Mitsuo Fuchida, the Japanese general commander who led the devastating attack on Pearl Harbor. He was a hero to the Japanese but hated by the Americans.

Shortly after the attack, Jake DeShazer enlisted in the U.S. Air Force with a personal vendetta against Commander Fuchida and the Japanese. He participated in Jimmy Doolittle's secret bombing raid over Tokyo some four months after Pearl Harbor. During the mission, his plane ran out of fuel and he was forced to land in Japanese-occupied China. He was captured by the Japanese and held as a prisoner of war for more than three years.

Close to death due to starvation and torture, DeShazer begged his captors for a Bible. After reading many passages, he gave his heart to God. "I suddenly discovered God had given me new spiritual eyes," he later said. "I found my bitter hatred for them [the Japanese] changed to loving pity."

DeShazer's new spiritual perspective gave him physical strength and purpose for living. When the war ended he was released and fully recovered. He returned to the U.S. and enrolled in a Bible college. Upon his graduation he returned to Japan, only this time he brought love and a message of hope instead of hatred.

Years later, Mitsuo Fuchida was stepping off a train in Tokyo when an American missionary handed him a pamphlet entitled, "I Was a Prisoner of Japan," written by DeShazer. Impressed with the peace DeShazer had found in Scripture, the desperately unhappy Fuchida purchased a Bible and began studying it. He was struck by the words of Jesus: "Father, forgive them, for they don't know what they are doing" (Luke 23:34). He realized he was one of those for whom Christ had prayed.

"I requested him to forgive my sins and change me from a bitter, disillusioned ex-pilot into a balanced person with purpose in living," he said. "I would give anything to retract my actions at Pearl Harbor . . . but it is impossible."

This man, who led the raid of death with a great ambition to become a highly acclaimed fighter pilot, spent the last twenty-five years of his life as an "ambassador of peace" sharing the message of forgiveness.[1]

Impossible as it may seem, God is able to reveal the truth of forgiveness of sins to the most hate-filled avenger and also to the most determined aggressor. He wants us to agree with his purposes and pray to that end.

PRAYER

Lord, although it's difficult to pray for our enemies, if they embraced your truth, they would cease being an enemy! Reveal the truth to them—as only you can. Amen.

Bring Good Out of Evil

———— 〰 ————

And we know that all things work together for good to those who love God, to those who are the called according to His purpose.

ROMANS 8:28

When catastrophe strikes at the hands of evil ones, we grope for answers. The act itself is so senseless that a satisfactory explanation eludes us. But can we possibly find some measure of good in the midst of such evil? Absolutely. There are notable examples in Scripture.

For example, Joseph, sold into slavery by his brothers, unfairly accused and imprisoned in Egypt, eventually became prime minister in the land of his exile. He was then able to save his people from starvation (Gen. 41). David was unjustly persecuted by the jealous, corrupt King Saul, yet the young shepherd trusted God to vindicate him, and in due time became king of Israel (2 Sam. 2). Stephen was martyred by religious authorities while Saul, one of the zealots, witnessed his death. Then Saul had a dramatic encounter with Christ and became the apostle Paul—who wrote more than half the New Testament (Acts 9).

One of my (Ruthanne) college classmates, Jay Tucker, was a career missionary to northeastern Congo. After being taken captive by fanatical revolutionaries during the Simba uprising, he was brutally beaten to death. A policeman in the village whom Jay had converted was forced into the gruesome task of throwing Jay's body into the Bomokande River. He retrieved Jay's wedding ring and returned it to his wife, Angeline. In both Africa and America, we grieved the loss of this gentle, loving man.

The river that became Jay's grave flows through the tribal lands of the Mangbeto, a people among whom all attempts to plant churches had failed. At about this time in the revolution, this same African policeman was assigned the task of trying to pacify the Mangbeto. As he worked among this fierce tribe he heard an unusual folk proverb repeated often: "We must hear the words of one whose blood has been spilled in our river."

Amazed, the policeman called the chief and his elders together, saying, "I know a man whose blood was shed in your river. He is not here to speak, but let me tell you the words he gave to me." For the first time, the tribesmen listened intently to the gospel. The policeman continued to share his faith. Today more than forty churches exist among the Mangbeto.

Jay Tucker's death was a cruel tragedy causing deep grief. God did not make it happen. But God used even such a tragedy for eternal good. Yes, good *can* come out of evil.[2]

〰️

PRAYER

Lord, it's hard to see how anything good could come out of the death and devastation we've seen in our country. Yet we have your promise that all things work together for good for those who love you. Help us to trust you to do a work of grace even in these circumstances. Amen.

Bring Them to Justice

———— ❧ ————

The Lord reigns forever;
He has established his throne for judgment.
He will judge the world in righteousness;
He will govern the peoples with justice.

PSALM 9:7–8

On the morning of September 11, theologian Miroslav Volf was speaking at a United Nations prayer breakfast a few blocks away from the World Trade Center. Born in Croatia, he had witnessed the bloody war between the Croats and Serbs. In a town near his own, thirty thousand people had been either killed or driven out. In a country of 4.5 million, close to a million became refugees.

Just one week after the attacks, in an interview with *Christianity Today*, Volf talked about a godly response to our nation's enemies. "The first thought on many of our minds was that such vicious acts demand revenge," he said. "On one level, there will be a gut reaction—a sense of rage. Rage is [a] natural first response. It is also an appropriate response if we do it before the God of infinite love and justice."[3]

That's what David did in many of his Psalms when writing about his enemies:

- "Strike them with terror, O Lord" (Ps. 9:20).
- "Break the arm of the wicked and evil man; call him to account for his wickedness" (Ps. 10:15).

- "Rise up, O Lord, confront them, bring them down; rescue me from the wicked by your sword" (Ps. 17:13).

When injustice is done to us, when innocent blood is shed senselessly, we cry out for justice—for vengeance and retribution. Volf advocates the radical, *biblical* response of reconciliation with our enemies. He said the gospel requires us to embrace our enemies and seek reconciliation. However, he said, that doesn't mean we should forgo justice.

"We have to protect ourselves from the possibility of such an event happening again," Volf said. "If you are certain they would repeat the act, trying to stop them may be required."[4]

But that won't bring back those who lost their lives. What about them? Their blood cries out for justice!

As David thought about his own enemies and the way they seemed to triumph, he wrote, "When I tried to understand all this, it was oppressive to me till I entered the sanctuary of God; then I understood their final destiny" (Ps. 73:16, 17).

We can be confident that, even if our enemies prevail, there will be ultimate justice one day. At the Last Judgment, each one of us will stand before the Righteous Judge as he metes out perfect justice. On that day, every knee will bow.

PRAYER

Lord, we don't always know how to mete out justice, but you do. You are the One who avenges all wrongdoing. Help us to go beyond our desire for revenge. As we pray for our enemies, we place our trust in you. Amen.

10

Praying for Personal Peace and Protection

I pray to God every night of my life to be given the strength and power to continue my efforts to inspire in others the interest, the obligation and the responsibilities that we owe to this land for the sake of future generations—for my boys and girls—so that we can always look back when the candle of life burns low and say, "Thank God I have contributed my best to the land that contributed so much to me."

EDWARD VERNON "EDDIE" RICKENBACKER,
CELEBRATED WORLD WAR I AMERICAN AVIATOR,
IN HIS BOOK *SEVEN CAME THROUGH*

When pilot Eddie Rickenbacker was forced to land his plane in the Pacific Ocean (during a World War II special mission) he and seven others drifted in a raft for twenty-four days, trying to survive in near hopeless conditions. Through his faith in God and strong leadership, he encouraged the others not to give up hope, and all of them survived. It's a good example for all of us.

Personal Protection

———— 〜 ————

The eternal God is your refuge,
And underneath are the everlasting arms.

DEUTERONOMY 33:27

Stanley was on the eighty-first floor of the World Trade Center south tower when Flight 175 struck that very floor. Diving under a desk, he started praying. When he looked up he actually saw a burning wing of the plane in the doorway of his department. But he could not get through the flaming rubble to the stairway—the remnant of an office wall blocked the way.

Now he was joined in prayer by an older man he could see beyond the wall. Stanley says that after prayer, "I felt as if a power came over me. I said to the wall, 'You're going to be no match for me and my Lord.'" Moments later he was able to punch through the wall and reach the other survivor. The two headed down the eighty-one flights, only to reach the concourse level and find it surrounded by fire. Wetting themselves under the sprinkler system, they held hands and ran through the flames to safety. First stop: Trinity Church, two blocks away, to give thanks!

But of course many did not survive. Richard Allen and Sean Booker, two friends working for the same company in the north tower, met every morning for prayer and Bible study in a ninety-ninth-floor storage room. Both men were Christian ministers for their respective churches. Family members said the quiet room was a place for reflection before they would go to their jobs on the ninety-third and ninety-eighth floors each morning. It's assumed that both men died in that room when Flight 11 crashed into the tower at about 8:45 A.M.

"Richie and Sean would always go in to work early," said Allen's mother. "Every morning, without fail, they would read the Bible and pray. I think they were doing that when they died. There's a reason God allowed this to happen."

But Sharon Booker, Sean's wife, still struggles. On that day she was at her new job in the Met Life building in midtown Manhattan. From her office she witnessed the airplane crashing into her husband's building. "You can't question God," she said. "But now I feel that when I leave the house I won't come back. I just want to feel peace and comfort, but I can't." She now grapples with the task of raising Sean's three surviving children.[1]

We can never comprehend why some people are spared from a disaster while others perish. A godly person has no guarantee that nothing bad will ever happen to him, but God can use every event, no matter how shattering, as raw material for fulfilling a higher, grander purpose that we cannot now perceive. Our comfort is that no matter what happens, God's arms are there to uphold us.

≈

PRAYER

Lord, when violence has ripped away my sense of security, I realize how dependent I am upon you. I run to you for refuge in these critical days. Amen.

My Struggle with Grief and Guilt

Surely our grief He Himself bore,
And our sorrows He carried.

ISAIAH 53:4A (NASB)

G rief and guilt are twin emotions that emerged the day the New York towers fell. Grief for those who died. Guilt experienced by those who survived.

One woman, a tourist in Manhattan who witnessed the collapse and heard the screams of people fleeing afterward said, "A piece of my soul died in that catastrophe; I will never be the same. I'm back home now. Safe. But it's very hard going back to the routine. I feel that I am dishonoring the memory of the victims; I feel unworthy of having been spared."[2]

Her sentiments have been echoed by many others, some of whom managed to escape from the upper floors of the towers. One burn victim we heard interviewed said, "I don't know why I was given another chance, but I want to make the most of it."

Not only did people feel guilty, but three quarters of Americans surveyed said they felt depressed for some days after the horrific event. "Americans are more saddened, more frightened, and more fatigued by what they are watching [on television] than was the case during the Gulf War," say researchers at the Pew Research Center. But the researchers also report a spiritual response across our country, with 69 percent of respondents saying they are praying more.[3]

How do we handle grief, whatever the circumstances? One way to find release for overwhelming emotions is simply to cry. Counselor Paula Sandford writes:

> I encourage you to let the tears flow when you have something to cry about, and not to believe anyone who tells you that grief and sorrow are a sign of lack of faith . . . The ability to cry is a gift of God. Those who receive that gift and allow it to work in them appropriately are much less likely to suffer from high blood pressure, ulcers, nervous breakdowns, or depression than those who suppress and control their emotions to put forward a courageous front . . . Emotional healing does not usually happen instantly. God respects your feelings; your need to grieve for a while.[4]

Guilt is also a natural emotion felt by those who survive, as they mentally rehearse over and over the ways they might have prevented the tragedy. Hopefully in time we can surrender these burdens of regret to the Lord through prayer. We must try to go on living in the present, and make our lives count.

~

PRAYER

Lord, help me bear the grief I feel in all the losses I've experienced. Show me how to release my guilt to you. Help me put my life back together and move forward. I need you more than ever to see me through this.

My Struggle with Fear

———— ❧ ————

The Lord is my light and my salvation.
Whom shall I fear?
The Lord is the stronghold of my life.
Of whom shall I be afraid? . . .
For in the day of trouble
He will keep me safe in his dwelling.

PSALM 27:1, 5

Fear. Dread. Alarm. Terror. How easy it is for us to feel engulfed by such feelings.

Faith. Confidence. Dependence on God. Trust without need of certain proof.

Which will you allow to grip you today? Fear or faith? Both believe something is going to happen. Fear believes something bad is going to happen. Faith believes something good or positive will happen.

Abraham Lincoln, during his circuit-riding days as a lawyer, traveled to various small towns where courts were held. Often this meant crossing rivers, including the notorious Fox River, which was turbulent and dangerous during heavy rains.

Once, after several difficult river crossings, Lincoln's companion said, "If these rivers are this bad, whatever will it be like when we must cross the Fox?"

At the inn where they stopped that night, they asked an itinerant minister if he'd had experience with the Fox River.

"Yes," he said. "I've discovered a secret about crossing

the Fox River which I never fail to keep in mind. It is this: I never cross the Fox River *until* I reach the Fox River."

Many in our nation seem plagued with fear of the future. We fear further acts of terrorism. We fear getting on an airplane. We fear losing our jobs and retirement benefits. We fear biological warfare, disease, or death.

Most of the time the things we fear don't happen to us—or when frightening things do occur, we discover that God's strength is able to help us endure. Here's a biblical antidote for fear: "Do not be anxious about anything, but in everything, by prayer and petition, with thanksgiving, present your requests to God. And the peace of God which transcends all understanding, will guard your hearts and minds in Christ Jesus" (Phil. 4:6-7).

In our fearful moments we can declare God's Word—even quoting it aloud—to remind ourselves that our God helps us overcome fear. He promises never to leave us nor forsake us (Heb. 13:5).

✍

PRAYER

Lord, help me learn that I should never cross rivers until I get to them. Thank you that, because of your promise, I don't have to live under a cloud of fear. I know your grace is sufficient for every need. Help me to put my complete trust in you. Amen.

My Struggle with Anger

---- ✐ ----

"Don't sin by letting anger gain control over you." Don't let the sun go down while you are still angry, for anger gives a mighty foothold to the Devil.

EPHESIANS 4:26-27 (NLT)

When we feel our rights have been violated, our anger quickly pops to the surface. Life's daily stresses sometimes push us to the boiling point, and we lose control. Instances of child abuse, spousal abuse, road rage, airport rage, and similar problems have skyrocketed in our society. Many people are so accustomed to having things go their way that they feel justified in displaying their anger when they don't.

Commentator William Barclay wrote:

The anger which is selfish and uncontrolled is a sinful and hurtful thing, which must be banished from the Christian life. But the selfless anger which is disciplined into the service of Christ and of our fellow men is one of the great dynamic forces of the world.[5]

Usually we think of anger as being a negative emotion. But we see in the life of Christ that He exhibited anger toward self-righteous religious people because they were polluting the Temple (Mark 11:15-17). His anger served a useful purpose.

A good example of anger directed toward a useful cause is the founding of Mothers Against Drunk Driving (MADD).

Can you imagine the anger a mother feels when her child is killed in a senseless accident because of a drunk driver? Especially when the driver survives the accident and receives such a light sentence he is soon free to drink and drive again.

This organization brings together parents who have suffered such a tragedy. Their anger is directed toward lobbying for laws to keep drunk drivers from getting behind the wheel so that our streets and highways are safer.

Many Americans have felt intensely angry after the unprovoked attacks on civilian targets in our country. We must take care to use this emotion constructively. One pastor put it this way:

> I am angry with the terrorists who committed such events. I am angry that innocent people were slaughtered. I am angry that our country was attacked . . . Yet I know that I cannot dwell in my anger. [It] must turn into a resolve to stand up for my country, but even more, my anger must become a resolve to turn wholeheartedly to God and to stand against evil of every kind. Anger cannot be my steady diet—I must live in faith . . . It is only as Christians kneeling in prayer that we can begin to solve the problems and heal the insanity before us.[6]

If we ask him, the Lord can help us find useful ways to channel our anger.

PRAYER

Lord, you see the anger I feel about the stresses in my life, and the injustices I see around me every day. Please forgive me, and help me release this anger to you. Thank you, Lord. Amen.

Strengthening My Faith

———— 〰 ————

I pray that out of his glorious riches he may strengthen you
with power through his Spirit in your inner being, so that
Christ may dwell in your hearts through faith.

EPHESIANS 3:16–17

What does it mean to trust God? Is it that we must believe his power will produce the ideal result we have
in mind? No, for that would mean believing in our solution,
not his.

Trusting him means believing in his wisdom to choose
better than we could choose and believing in his power to
accomplish that divine purpose. As a well-loved child will
trust his mother's wisdom even when it contradicts his own,
the believer who knows God's love will rest securely, trusting
even when he does not understand.

How do you maintain faith when all around you things
are falling apart? One author suggests:

When the darkness comes into our lives, when light
seems to vanish and we begin to feel as though the sun
will never break the heaviness of our night, that is the
time to "trust in the name of the Lord." That is the
time to rely on our God and wait for Him. Those who
scramble around trying to manufacture their own light
and comfort, apart from God, will only find hurt and
sorrow at the end of the trail . . . What are some of the
"torches" we use to light our own way when the dark-

ness or circumstances closes in around us? . . . The pursuit of pleasure. Frantic activity. Workaholism. Chasing money and "things." Alcohol or drugs. Running after shallow, ungodly relationships . . . What do we do in the darkness? Trust God for protection. We trust God to deliver us. We wait on God to give us direction and lead us out of our cave and into His sunlight.[7]

Opportunities come our way almost every day to test our faith. One couple we know, Pam and Chuck, wanted to be parents in the worst way. Fertility specialists gave them little hope. Finally, after seven years of trying, they adopted a baby boy. Then, you guessed it—Pam became pregnant. Her unplanned pregnancy should have been a source of great joy, but it was plagued with problems.

"I entered the darkest period of my life. All I could do was to continue putting my faith in God," she said. When she had nightmares about her baby being born with physical deformities, she would reach out in faith to God and go back to sleep. Finally, after months of physical problems, Rebecca was born perfectly healthy.

Four years later Pam gave birth to identical twin boys, but both babies died within a few days. In the midst of her grief, she could declare, without a trace of bitterness, "Yet will I trust him." Eventually she had four more healthy children, despite the fact doctors had said it was impossible.[8]

Pam strengthened her faith through the Word of God and prayer. Every time the enemy assaulted her mind with doubt she found comfort in Scripture. Each time she prayed, the Holy Spirit led her to relevant passages that would reinforce her determination to trust God through every test.

These sources are available to every one of us. Like Pam, we can discover that the testing of our faith ultimately can lead to the strengthening of our faith.

PRAYER

Father, forgive me for the times I've failed to trust you. Help me to reach a higher level of faith and trust in you. Amen.

11

How to Pray Effectively

One of the greatest drawbacks to the life of prayer is that the answer does not come as quickly as we expect. We are discouraged and think: "Perhaps I do not pray right." So we do not persevere. Jesus often talked about this. There may be a reason for the delay and the waiting may bring a blessing. Our desire must grow deeper and stronger, and we must ask with our whole heart. God puts us into the practicing school of persevering prayer so that our weak faith may be strengthened.

Above all God wants to draw us into closer fellowship with Him. When our prayers are not answered we learn that the fellowship and love of God are more to us than the answers of our requests, and then we continue in prayer.

ANDREW MURRAY, FROM *THE BEST OF
ANDREW MURRAY ON PRAYER*

When the apostle Paul was approaching the end of his life he wrote this to Timothy, whom he had mentored: "I have fought the good fight, I have finished the race, I have kept the faith. Now there is in store for me the crown of righteousness" (1 Tim. 4:7-8a). To start a race is one thing, but the goal is to finish despite all setbacks. We are setting out with a new determination to pray for our nation as never before. May we not drop out of the race.

Praying in Agreement
with God's Word

———— ✎ ————

For the word of God is living and active and sharper than any two-edged sword . . . piercing as far as the division of soul and spirit . . . able to judge the thoughts and intentions of the heart.

HEBREWS 4:12 (NASB)

The above verse clearly illustrates that God's Word reveals the motives of our hearts. As we study the Scriptures, God can show us the attitudes we need to change in order to be more like him. Our *lives* should be in agreement—or in harmony—with God's Word so that our *prayers* can be effective.

One way to be sure our prayers are aligned with the will of God is to pray directly from Scriptures. Jesus himself gave us an example. During his youth, he studied Scripture and filled his mind with its truth. Therefore, when the devil tempted him in the wilderness, Jesus' sword was sharp and ready. He used his Father's Word to defeat the enemy by declaring, "It is written, 'Man shall not live on bread alone'" (Luke 4:4). With this statement he acknowledged the power of Scripture.

With God's Word, the strongest weapon in our spiritual arsenal, we can turn difficulties into opportunities. God spoke this promise through the prophet Isaiah: "So is my word that goes out from my mouth: It will not return to me empty, but will accomplish what I desire and achieve the purpose for which I sent it" (Isa. 55:11).

I (Quin) spent many days and nights walking the floor, praying for my prodigal children to come back to the faith from which they had strayed. "It is written!" I declared as I paraphrased various portions of Scripture: "The seeds of the righteous shall be delivered . . . My children shall be taught of the Lord, and great will be their peace . . . Thank you, Lord, that you will give your angels charge over my children to guard them in all their ways" (Prov. 11:21; Isa. 54:13; Ps. 91:11). I took comfort in the fact that God promises his Word is true and I believed he would answer me. And I was rewarded: after five years of constant prayer all three of my children returned to the Lord within an eight-month period.

As you prayerfully study God's Word, allow him to lead you to the Scriptures that will aid you in your own situation. Be open to his guidance. And pray with confidence.

PRAYER

Lord, thank you for the Bible, which is packed with wonderful promises. Please show me the passages I need to pray for the circumstances I am facing. Thank you for answering my prayer in your time, in your way—which is always best. Amen.

Finding a Prayer Partner

If two of you on earth agree about anything you ask for, it will be done for you by my Father in heaven. For where two or three come together in my name, there am I with them.

MATTHEW 18:19

How do we participate in this call to prayer as we cry out for God to be with us? One way is to pray individually and privately. Another is to pray in agreement with others in a prayer partnership.

As the enormity of the attack on our nation began to sink in, millions of people became aware of the need to pray and a desire to meet with others of like mind. In cities across America churches opened their doors for prayer. People gathered to pray on street corners, in parks, offices, factories, stores, and homes. They instinctively sought each other out and were comforted by the togetherness of shared prayer.

Prayer partnerships are made up of people who pray together for similar concerns and goals—intercessors who stand in the prayer gap for others. Some may be hesitant to appear vulnerable before others—to share confidences with another person. Yet those who have had long-term prayer partnerships attest to the strength and encouragement they've experienced.

How do you find a prayer partner? Begin praying with your spouse or a close friend. Ask God to lead you to someone of his choosing. Most likely you'll find a prayer partner within your church, your family, your workplace, or your neighborhood. Because prayer partners form close bonds, it's best to have a prayer partner of the same sex, unless of course you are praying with your spouse. Trust the words of Matthew 18:19 written above. The word *agree*—derived from a root from which we get the word *symphony*—means to be of one mind and purpose, or to be in harmony. God can help you find someone to harmonize with in prayer.

I (Quin) know of a family prayer partnership consisting of a mother and her three adult daughters. One Sunday afternoon of each month they spend time praying for their large, extended family. Two of the sisters drive seventy miles each way for this gathering. They have reported many prayers answered—especially regarding the reconciliation of several family members—as they've prayed together for more than a year. Now their aunts and cousins call them to ask for prayer.

I myself prayed with my friend Lib for our seven children for five minutes on the phone at 8:00 A.M. every weekday morning for seventeen years. Additionally, every morning my husband and I pray together asking for the Lord's presence, power, provision, protection, and direction for our children and grandchildren. We pray for their peers, teachers, and employers. We pray for our pastor and his family. We pray for our president and government leaders. We pray for friends and neighbors.

Take up the challenge of praying with a prayer partner. It's a rewarding adventure.

PRAYER

Lord, direct me to the right person to form a prayer partnership. I want to deepen my prayer life and strengthen my faith. Please help me. Amen.

Remaining Steadfast and Focused

---- ✦ ----

Create in me a pure heart, O God,
And renew a steadfast spirit within me . . .
Grant me a willing spirit, to sustain me.

PSALM 51:10, 12b

Are we steadfast in our prayer life? Immovable? Determined? Resolved? Focused? We must be if we are to pray effectively for our family, our community, and our nation. Yet as we grow in the process of praying for others, God may well show us a need for some attitude adjustments—some heart changes needed so that we may pray with the right motives in mind.

Many of us watched Franklin Graham, son of evangelist Billy Graham, on television from New York as he reported how some of his coworkers had set up a relief station near Ground Zero to minister to the rescuers still working at the disaster site. However, not everyone may know his personal story. He is now an ordained minister, but for many years he was considered the rebel of the family. Many prayers were offered for many years on his behalf, that he would return to God's fold.

Franklin's mother, Ruth Bell Graham, remembers one specific night when she was praying for her "lost lamb," as she called him. As she usually did, she slipped to her knees to once again commit Franklin to the Lord. But this time she said she realized she must first "commit what was left of me to God." In other words, she had to let go and trust in God. She did this, then sought God's response.

"He impressed me, 'You take care of the possible, and trust me for the impossible,'" she said.

Of course her prayers—and those of many others—were answered in time. On the day of Franklin's ordination, his mother shared this story and added, "Today you are seeing the impossible."[1]

During a time I (Quin) was praying for my own son to turn back to the Lord, I was particularly concerned about one of his peers, who I felt was a bad influence on my son. I strongly believed they needed to be separated from each other, and I was praying for that. Then one night my eyes were riveted by a particular Bible verse: "God turned—or broke—Job's captivity when he prayed for his friends" (Job 42:10 KJV).

I realized I needed to change my prayers—that I needed to pray God's blessings for the young man who was having such an adverse influence on my son, just as much as I was praying for my own child. Therefore, several times each day my husband and I prayed that God would bless this young man and help him fulfill his destiny. Within a short time he was awarded a college scholarship in another state and he moved.

God did fulfill his purpose for this young man through his schooling, and eventually through his choice of a career. In the meantime, God changed my own heart and prayers—in the boy's favor.

If we give God permission, he often changes our prayers midcourse, as if to say, "Have you considered this, my child?"

Give him the chance to do so if he desires. You might be surprised by the results!

PRAYER

Lord, help me stay steadfast and focused in my prayers. Thank you for the ways you have already answered prayers. Please teach me how to pray more effectively. Thank you for your mercy, love, and guidance. Amen.

Praying Unselfish Prayers

——————— ∾ ———————

Our Father, which art in heaven,
Hallowed be thy name.
Thy kingdom come,
Thy will be done on earth
As it is in heaven.
Give us this day our daily bread.
And forgive us our debts,
As we forgive our debtors.
And lead us not into temptation,
But deliver us from evil.
For thine is the kingdom, and the power, and the glory,
    for ever. Amen.

MATTHEW 6:9–13 (NASB)

This prayer, known as The Lord's Prayer, is our guide for unselfish praying. We begin by acknowledging that God is our heavenly father, and we affirm his holiness. We pray for his will to be done on earth—in our own neighborhood, city, and nation, and in the nations of the world. And we agree with him that we also want his will in our individual lives.

Praying for God's kingdom to come on earth takes precedence over praying for our physical needs. It's interesting that the petition for "daily bread"—symbolizing everything necessary to sustain our physical beings—is the shortest sentence in this prayer. Yes, God is concerned about our needs, but he wants us to see the bigger picture.

We ask for God's forgiveness because only he can forgive sins. But to receive this gift we must forgive all those we have grievances against. It's a condition for having our sins forgiven.

Take, for instance, the prayer Jesus uttered during the crucifixion. Never has a more unselfish prayer been voiced than the one he gave from the cross as people watched and rulers sneered. Though in severe pain, he looked down on them and cried, "Father, forgive them!" (Luke 23:34).

Unselfish prayers are given for people other than ourselves. Another term for it is *intercessory prayer*—prayer motivated by an unselfish attitude of servanthood. Have you thought about praying for the burn victims of the terrorists' hit? For the pastors and counselors who have spent endless hours helping trauma victims? For those orphaned or widowed by the attack on our nation? For those left without jobs following the devastation? Have you thought about praying for the Afghan refugees?

As you take the time to consider others, your list of intercessory prayer needs will grow. Look around your own neighborhood or town—are there those who would benefit from your prayers? What about beyond the boundaries of your city? Ask God for a specific prayer assignment as you watch the news, read the newspaper, or listen to the radio. As you remain sensitive to God's directions names and events will pierce your hearts and call you to prayer.

A friend of ours prays every day: "Lord, please order every detail, every contact, every conversation, every point of communication today, according to your divine order." Because of her openness, God causes her to meet all kinds of people in the most unusual ways, and she prays for them long after she's met them. Hers is an unselfish lifestyle of prayer.

We trust you will take up the challenge and join your voice in prayer with others across America as we implore, "God be with us."

PRAYER

Lord, there are so many needs in the world. Please show me my specific prayer assignment. I want to see your will done throughout the earth, and also in my own life. Amen.

It Is Well with My Soul

Horatio G. Spafford, a loyal friend and supporter of evangelist D. L. Moody, suffered enormous trauma and loss in his life. Most of his family's assets were wiped out in the great Chicago fire of 1871. In November 1873, wanting to lift his family's spirits, he planned to take them on an overseas vacation that would include attending Mr. Moody's evangelistic campaign in Great Britain.

At the last minute Mr. Spafford had to tend to urgent business, but he sent his wife and four daughters as scheduled on the S.S. *Ville de Havre*, expecting to join them later. Midway across the Atlantic, their ship collided with an English ship and sank within minutes. All four Spafford daughters perished among the 226 lost at sea. Miraculously, Anna Spafford was one of the few survivors. She sent her husband the now-famous telegram message: "Saved alone."

Several weeks later, as Spafford stood on the deck of a ship carrying him to Wales to meet Anna, he passed the spot where his children had died. Inspired by the Holy Spirit, he wrote the words that have comforted believers in times of grief for more than a hundred years. The melody, composed by Philip Paul Bliss in 1876, was named "Ville de Havre" after the ship on which Spafford's children died.[1]

It Is Well with My Soul

When peace, like a river, attendeth my way,
When sorrows like sea billows roll;

Whatever my lot, Thou has taught me to say,
It is well, it is well, with my soul.

Though Satan should buffet, though trials should come,
Let this blessed assurance control,
That Christ has regarded my helpless estate,
And hath shed His own blood for my soul.

My sin, oh, the bliss of this glorious thought!
My sin, not in part but the whole,
Is nailed to the cross, and I bear it no more,
Praise the Lord, praise the Lord, O my soul!

And Lord, haste the day when my faith shall be sight,
The clouds be rolled back as a scroll;
The trump shall resound, and the Lord shall descend,
Even so, it is well with my soul.

It is well, with my soul,
It is well, it is well, with my soul.[2]

NOTES

CHAPTER 1

1. *USA Today*, September 21, 2001.

2. *People Weekly,* September 24, 2001 (Vol. 56, No. 13), 116, 132.

3. "'Prayer is our hope line,' pastor tells New Yorkers," Susan Barton, *North Texas United Methodist Review*, September 28, 2001 (Vol. 4, No. 8), 1.

4. *People Weekly,* September 24, 2001 (Vol. 56, No. 13), 128.

5. Adapted from *Our National Anthem* by Stephanie St. Pierre, (Brookfield, CT: Millbrook Press, 1992), 16–20; and *America's God and Country Encyclopedia of Quotations,* William J. Federer, ed. (Fame Publishing, 1996), 351.

6. "The Star Spangled Banner," Sir Francis Scott Key, 1814.

7. Philip Yancey, *Finding God in Unexpected Places* (Ann Arbor, MI: Servant, 1997), 92.

8. "And Can It Be," Charles Wesley, 1738.

9. Elisabeth Elliot, *On Asking God Why* (Old Tappan, NJ: Revell, 1989), 18.

10. Adapted from *A Woman's Guide to Getting Through Tough Times*, by Quin Sherrer and Ruthanne Garlock, (Ann Arbor, MI: 1998), 212-214.

CHAPTER 2

1. Adapted from *Miracles Happen When You Pray*, by Quin Sherrer (Grand Rapids, MI: Zondervan, 1997), 143-144.

2. From a personal interview with Ruthanne Garlock. The subject's name has been changed. Used by permission.

3. *The Book of Common Prayer* (New York: The Seabury Press, 1979).

4. As quoted in *USA Today,* Sept. 21, 2001, from the *Daily Illini,* University of Illinois, Champaign, IL.

5. From an interview on the *CBS Early Show,* September 13, 2001, in a piece entitled "Where Is God?" taken from <www.cbsnews.com/earlyshow>.

CHAPTER 3

1. "America the Beautiful," Katherine Lee Bates, 1893.

2. Kenneth W. Osbeck, *101 More Hymn Stories* (Grand Rapids, MI: Kregel Publishing, 1985), 34-35.

3. Lew Brodsky, a senior Selective Service Official, as quoted by the Associated Press in the *Denver Post*, September 30, 2001.

4. Ibid.

5. "Eternal Father, Strong to Save," William Whiting, 1860.

6. "Precious Mettle," *People Weekly,* October 1, 2001 (Vol. 56, No. 14), 22-24.

7. "Honoring the Fallen, Comforting Their Friends," *People Weekly,* October 1, 2001 (Vol. 56, No. 14), 71.

8. *People Weekly,* October 1, 2001 (Vol. 56, No. 14), 29.

9. *People Weekly,* October 1, 2001 (Vol. 56, No. 14), 30.

10. Douglas Connelly, *Wisdom from a Pastor's Heart* (San Francisco, CA: Jossey-Bass, 2001), 186.

11. *People Weekly,* October 1, 2001 (Vol. 56, No. 14.), 96.

CHAPTER 4

1. "Operation Courage," an interview with H. Norman Schwarzkopf, *Leadership Journal,* Fall 1997.

2. Ibid.

3. *America's God and Country Encyclopedia of Quotations,* William J. Federer, ed. (Fame Publishing, 1996), 226.

4. Cindy Loose and Gary Lee, "The Skies of America Closed," *The Washington Post,* September 16, 2001, E01.

5. *World Fact Book.* Washington, D.C.: Central Intelligence Agency, 2000; Bartleby.com, 2000.

CHAPTER 5

1. Adapted from *A Woman's Guide to Getting Through Tough Times*, by Quin Sherrer and Ruthanne Garlock, (Ann Arbor, MI: 1998), 34-35.

CHAPTER 6

1. Kenneth Barker, Gen. Ed., *The NIV Study Bible*, (Grand Rapids, MI: Zondervan, 1985), commentary on Romans 13:1, page 2190.

2. "Mayors on Front Line in National Response," compiled by Will McMaster and Chris Berry, *U.S. Mayor,* September 24, 2001.

3. Wendy Murray Zoba, "More than a Badge and a Gun," *Christianity Today*, October 23, 2000.

4. Ibid.

5. *Firefighter's Quarterly Magazine,* online at <www.fdny.net>.

CHAPTER 7

1. Dutch Sheets, *The Beginners Guide to Intercession* (Ann Arbor, MI: Servant, 2001), 171.

2. Taken from <www.dutchsheets.org>.

3. *The Book of Common Prayer*.

4. Taken from an interview with Ruthanne Garlock. Used by permission.

5. Jamie MacDonald, as quoted in "We Shall Overcome," Kenneth Auchincloss, *Newsweek Special Report* magazine, Sept. 24, 2001, 20.

6. Craig Brian Larson, ed., "Illustrations for Preaching and Teaching," *Leadership Journal* (Grand Rapids, MI: Baker Books, 1993), 111.

7. *People Weekly,* October 1, 2001 (Vol. 56, No. 14), 72.

CHAPTER 8

1. "A Report from Ground Zero," interview with Rick Leventhal taken from <www.foxnews.com>.

2. Adapted from *A Woman's Guide to Getting Through Tough Times*, by Quin Sherrer and Ruthanne Garlock (Ann Arbor, MI: 1998) 199-200.

3. Diane Huie Balay, "Airline personnel stand on faith in attacks' aftermath," *North Texas United Methodist Review* (PO Box 660275, Dallas, TX 75266), 2.

4. Taken from <www.syatp.com/pages/0922.htm>.

5. Information from The Call New England Offices in West Haven, CT; <www.thecallne.org>.

6. *The Journals of Rachel Scott*, adapted by Beth Nimmo and Debra K. Klingsporn (Nashville: Tommy Nelson, a division of Thomas Nelson, Inc., 2001), 119.

7. Taped message by Pastor Bruce Porter of Celebration Christian Church, Littleton, Colorado, June 1, 1999.

8. Adapted from *Prayer Partnerships* by Quin Sherrer and Ruthanne Garlock (Ann Arbor, MI: Servant, 2001), 105.

CHAPTER 9

1. Dr. John Paul Loucky, "From Pearl Harbor to Calvary." Adapted and used by permission. The English version of this story with vocabulary notes appeared in Dr. Loucky's *Famous Leaders Who Influenced Japan's Internationalization* (1994). Fuchida's complete biography, *God's Samurai: Lead Pilot at Pearl Harbor*, was written by Gordon W. Prange (Washington, DC: Brassey's, 1990).

2. Adapted from *Pentecostal Evangel,* January 10, 1993 (Springfield, Mo: Assemblies of God).

3. "To Embrace the Enemy," an interview with Miroslav Volf, *Christianity Today*, September 17, 2001.

4. Ibid.

CHAPTER 10

1. "Families reflect on their losses," *Chicago Tribune*, September 24, 2001, Section 1, page 10.

2. Pam Baugh Walsh, *San Antonio Express News*, September 30, 2001, Section G, page 1.

3. *The Washington Post* article reprinted in *The Gazette*, Colorado Springs, CO., October 1, 2001, Life Section, page 4.

4. Paula Sandford, *Healing Women's Emotions* (Tulsa, OK: Victory House, 1992), 39, 82.

5. William Barclay, *The Letters to the Galatians and Ephesians*, rev. ed. (Philadelphia: Westminster, 1976), 156.

6. Chris Allen, "Pray for Our Country—Pray for Us," *North Texas United Methodist Review*, Tyler Street UMC edition, September 28, 2001, 1.

7. Ron Mehl, *God Works the Night Shift* (Sisters, OR: Multnomah Books, 1994), 130.

8. Adapted from *A Woman's Guide to Getting Through Tough Times,* 160-166.

CHAPTER 11

1. Ruth Bell Graham, "A Mother's View," *Christian Life* Magazine, November 1984, 52.

IT IS WELL WITH MY SOUL

1. Taken from *Amazing Grace: 366 Inspiring Hymn Stories for Daily Devotions,* by Kenneth W. Osbeck (Grand Rapids: Kregel, 1990), 202; and from the Music for the Church of God website at <www.cgmusic.com/cghymnal>.

2. "It Is Well with My Soul," Horatio Gates Spafford, 1873.